Beyond
Liberalism,
Where
Relations
Grow

the text of this book is printed
on 100% recycled paper

BEYOND LIBERALISM, WHERE RELATIONS GROW

Henry S. Kariel
University of Hawaii

HARPER COLOPHON BOOKS
Harper & Row, Publishers
New York, Hagerstown, San Francisco, London

Previously published and copyrighted materials are included with the kind permission of authors, publishers, or copyright owners as listed below:

Michel Foucault. *The Order of Things*. Translated by Alan Sheridan Smith. Copyright © 1970 by Pantheon Books, a division of Random House, Inc. Used by permission. Quoted herein at p. 69.

Clifford Geertz. *The Interpretation of Cultures*. Copyright © 1973 by Basic Books, Inc., Publishers, New York. From pp. 403-404. Used by permission. Quoted herein at pp. 104-105.

Peter Marin. "Tripping the Heavy Fantastic." *The New York Times Book Review*, February 21, 1971; p. 7. Copyright © 1971 by The New York Times Company. Reprinted by permission. Quoted herein at pp. 32, 46.

Morse Peckham. Reprinted from *The Triumph of Romanticism*, edited by Morse Peckham, pp. 55-57, by permission of the University of South Carolina Press. Copyright © 1970 by University of South Carolina Press.

Morse Peckham. Delivered at the annual meeting of the American Psychological Association, September, 1966. First published in *Literature and Psychology*, XVI (Spring, 1966). Reprinted by permission from *The Triumph of Romanticism* (University of South Carolina Press, 1970). Copyright © 1966 by Leonard F. Manheim and Morton Kaplan. Copyright © 1970 by University of South Carolina Press.

Harold Rosenberg. *Art on the Edge*. New York: Macmillan, 1975; pp. 18-19. Copyright © 1974-1975 by Harold Rosenberg. Originally appeared in *The New Yorker*. Used by permission. Quoted herein at p. 85.

Richard Sennett and Jonathan Cobb. *The Hidden Injuries of Class*. Copyright © 1972 by Alfred A. Knopf, Inc. Used by permission. Quoted herein at pp. 14, 30, 118.

Orion White, Jr. *Psychic Energy and Organizational Change*. Copyright © 1973 by Sage Publications, Inc.; pp. 30-34, reprinted by permission of the publishers, Sage Publications, Inc. A Sage Professional Paper in Administrative and Policy Studies, #03-007. Quoted from a lecture at Syracuse University, 1971. Quoted herein at pp. 96-97.

Alfred Willener. *The Action-Image of Society*. Translated by Alan Sheridan Smith. New York: Pantheon Books, Inc., 1970; pp. 239, 258-259, 264-266, 277. Reprinted by permission of Tavistock Publications, Ltd. Quoted herein at pp. 63-65, 76; also see p. 67.

For Sasha
who has lived this book with me

Contents

Prefatory Note

Making my daily rounds, I know too well that I do not find myself whirling in some postliberal world of infinite possibilities. I earn my keep and move sensibly within the grid of liberalism. Mainly I teach college classes, write sentences that move predictably from subject to predicate, and check my shopping list before I take groceries from supermarket shelves. Even between bathhouse and beach I walk the shortest distance. And when I somehow stray from these comfortable routines, I am kept straight by an implacable metaphysics which assures me of the ultimate futility of every expressive gesture. There would appear to be no way out of the liberal world.

Yet while all this is clear and comforting, I recall moments of madness that have enhanced my sensible existence. At the edge of time I serve so well, I recurrently find myself in unaccredited situations and experience excitements which, as I know at the very time, are fuller—more full of suspense and drama—than anything scheduled on my appointment calendar. It may happen quite simply. The wrong ingredient in an omelette has turned out to be

---

There is no revolution; there are only revolutionary moments. These we have to perpetuate. That is what he said when they met the last time.

—Horst Bienek*

---

the right one: a sensible meal has turned into a feast, an exception into a rule. Of course, even as the feast keeps moving, even as it becomes an interminable festival, nothing finally comes of it. In fact, I am just more worn out. Yet though it is surely a time of inconsequence and futility, none who partici-

*Notes and Sources follow Chapter 9.

pate seek to bring the action to an end. On the contrary, they call their friends
to extend the life of the party. They keep contributing more of themselves,
begin to play new parts, try to act as chef, piano player, dishwasher, story
teller, or fool. They seek no end to this time of inconsequence.

In short, at the fringe of our well-planned projects—careers and marriages, trips and vacations—there are mad, useless intervals which intimate
what we are really after. I think it is possible to extend these intervals by
taking note, in my case at book length, of their essential sanity.

Perceiving cracks in the walls of the edifice of an individualistic
liberalism, we can inquire how to free energies repressed inside. How might
we raise existing discontents to the level of consciousness, widen the cracks,
and welcome alternatives? How might we change the patterns of our lives and
thereby develop resources for action? These have suddenly become timely
questions. History itself would seem to pose them.

> We are not victims of perfectible weaknesses in the social structure. Our humanity
> is being consumed by the structure itself: by the ruling constituents—the insti-
> tutions, the relationships, the consciousness, and the ideology—of the process that
> contains modern America. Our possibilities and our awareness of possibility are
> mutilated by the growing strength and effectiveness of that process. Our afflictions
> cannot be subdued by repairs or modifications, by those adjustments we call
> "reforms." For us, a political faith is not a useful and salutary illusion—it is an
> accomplice in oppression. If we wish to be freed, then, we must reject a stable
> tranquility—the calm acceptance of "realities" that are not real—in favor of
> defiance, outrage, and conflict. New accommodations with the dominant sources
> of social power will not alter our condition, diminish alienation, or amplify
> freedom. Power itself, the command over social resources, must be transferred and
> redesigned.[1]*

In the midst of *New Yorker* ads for diamonds and gin, a decade after having
served President Kennedy as speechwriter, Richard Goodwin insists that
power itself must be transferred and redesigned.

But how? No science of politics seems available for coping with the predicaments of the technologically advanced parts of the world. The frameworks of political scientists fail to frame our troubles. Not only are political
scientists betrayed by their chosen careers but their theories do not touch the
terrifying highs and lows of American life. Exhilarating as well as depressing
experiences remain unconnected. The private, self-denying language of the
social sciences is matched, it would seem, by artistic ventures: novelists,
movie directors, playwrights, painters, and poets seem to be equally unable to
make explicit the distinctively *political* dimensions of their works. Neither
social scientists nor artists create public structures for the feelings they
release, the malaise they exploit, the little excitements they keep generating.
Nor do journalists, culture critics, social commentators, and political

*Notes and Sources follow Chapter 9.

polemicists; they fastidiously document prevailing miseries but fail to relate them to the underlying forces of political life.

Because we seem near the end of usable rituals, myths, and languages, and because the strain is showing, this should be an auspicious time to inquire how we might be able to come to terms not only with the surface facts of American life—of political life generally in technologically sophisticated societies—but also with the suppressed, deflected, and ultimately wasted impulses at the political margin where public transactions fade into our unshared private lives. What language, what *form* of action, might enable us to comprehend and salvage experiences that keep eluding comprehension? How can we relate phenomena that strike us as unrelated, disconnected,

---

The nation's response to the attempted takeover of the nation by the executive branch is to increase the power of the executive branch; its response to being deceived on an unprecedented scale is to increase government secrecy; and its response to abuses of secret-police power is to issue to the secret police a license for even wider action. More profound, almost, than the question of where the country is now heading, therefore, is the question of whether any possible experience is left that can serve as a warning, or whether the country is simply immune to experience.

—*The New Yorker*, April 26, 1976

---

shocking, absurd, inexplicable, perverse, and unspeakable, which take possession of us, which leave us at the end of our wits, paralyzed or frenzied—in any case, uncommunicative and impotent?

In search of some defensible ground for effective public action, I am initially concerned with making the prevailing political formula explicit—that is, with giving the fullest possible recognition to what I have found easy to call the Myth of the Liberal Enlightenment. Further, I would want to make explicit what it has meant to implement the Liberal Myth—how ingeniously it has arrested individual and social development either by keeping us gently depressed or else by provoking mindless reactions on the Left and Right.

If the result of all this has been one or another escape from politics, the escapes may nevertheless be seen as political, as desperate efforts to communicate a faith in some ineffable larger whole, in some open-ended community within which people might quite legitimately relate and integrate progressively more aspects of their experience and *lead* richer lives. Because this interest in self-expansion is given a coherent basis in the aesthetic theory of Romanticism, I should like to enlist this theory to elaborate a basis for moving ahead.

All this, clearly, is risky advocacy, but not unthinkable once we shift the terms of our thinking. I would argue—near the edge of plausibility—that it is possible to stake out new political ground and that this effort itself can serve to renew the individual, his family, and his associations. To defend this position I would rely on nothing more than our irrepressible disposition to express ourselves by continuously jeopardizing whatever routines, creeds, and establishments emerge in the social landscape and fix themselves in the human mind. To vindicate ground for creative political action beyond liberalism requires no more, I think, than a defense of extending the self-expressive process of the arts to all spheres of our existence.

I am considerably less worried about failing in such an enterprise than I am about the persistence of a need-frustrating, death-dealing society that recurrently succeeds in doing *more*—that furnishes more solid goods, more benign banalities, more solemn truths, and more weighty grounds for enduring. In view of the embarrassing successes of liberalism, my main worry is that my own failure, especially my failure to conclude, may turn out to be excessively modest.

H. S. K.

Acknowledgments

I am grateful to all who participated in this project by questioning and supporting it, especially to participants in two seminars of mine, one at Hebrew University of Jerusalem and the other at the University of Hawaii, and no less to Robert S. Cahill, Reuel Denney, Harry J. Friedman, James Dator, and Michael J. Shapiro. Ernest Sneidman generously welcomed me to his retreat, a cabin on the slopes of Mt. Haleakala on the island of Maui, so that I might work on this volume. He was the most self-effacing patron I have ever had. Moreover, I was granted the opportunity to keep reworking my sentences in a setting which came excruciatingly close to actualizing my ideal beyond liberalism: I spent a month as scholar-in-residence at the Rockefeller Foundation's Villa Serbelloni.

Overlooking the village of Bellagio on Lake Como, the hillside villa has been placed in a landscape carefully designed to look what is called Italian. The floor-to-ceiling window of the suite I occupied frames a lovingly painted canvas of houses and chapels, of olive, pine, and cypress trees—all linked by winding roads and walls. The lake would seem to be but another artifact: it curves gently around terraced land which rises in the distance to form mountain ranges which in turn are encircled by snow-covered alps. Occasional October rains and varying cloud effects only add to the pervasive unreality of this composition. In fact, the landscape is as unreal, as much a product of a collective fantasy, as the villa and the life within it. Some dozen visiting scholars play the role of guest. They are aided by the resident director and his wife, William and Betsy Olson. The Olsons, supported by a cast of butlers and maids, footmen and cooks, gardeners and watchmen, meticulously set the stage and unobtrusively keep the play in motion. Their main concern—and in this they reveal an appealing detachment from the liberal ethos which I am questioning in this book—is not to mobilize the guests of the Rockefeller Foundation so that some worthy work might come of it all. Rather, it is to make sure that the show will go on. All act convincingly as if they saw the final value of their activities in nothing but an endless process. The villa, like the surrounding landscape, needs no purpose. For all but the less fortunate supporting cast—a third world for which life is *no* game—the villa is its own excuse for being.

For me, it is easy to follow the cue of E. M. Forster and give the villa two cheers—one for nourishing body and soul far beyond the needs of bare subsistence and the other for providing an ambience so stunningly artificial that it served me as continuous reminder of my own obligation to keep playing and performing—in a word, to remain political. The third cheer I reserve for the republic of love, for that holy place where, impassioned and without thought of etiquette, we wholly *care* for one another and where, as it happens, lies the only source of energy for the games that scholars play.

It is not quiet in the morning: there are cows, children, bike bells, music, the family below us, street vendors, loud, loud crows, some cars. But I've learned to concentrate. The trick of concentration is not shutting things out but letting them come through. So I let all this noise come through, and it passes through me as if it were sea water and I were a fishnet—only the biggest things get caught, set off chains of associations. I sing a little, just a little.

—Richard Schechner, *Environmental Theater* (1973)

Part One

The Governing Grid

"I'm still looking," she said. "Someone sure of himself."

"Jim was like that. He used to have lots of drive. Hot for certainties. Knew where he was headed and knew what was right. Worked on himself and straightened out the company. Kept working on me too. Always judging and doing things. Lots of excitement, but hard to take. Of course, he still knows what's right, but he's no longer sure. All the energy and toughness have gone out of him. Easier to live with though."

"But I'm looking for someone who's not judgmental at all."

1

The Dominant Myth

Critics of American institutions learn quickly when they are out of bounds. Their editors remind them of their obscure writing. Their readers misunderstand. In fact, the critics themselves become aware of their failure to respond to their own deepest impulses: they realize they do not act on their inner voice of dissent. They feel as if by instinct the extent to which prevailing beliefs validate their labors. Theirs is a familiar if poignant fate: yearning for a new society, they remain confined by the old. Thus even when enraged by what they depict, they keep their work free from tremors. The television camera recording the ugly interrogation of a prisoner is held steady: even though it expresses the cameraman's trained point of view, it does not betray his feelings. To be heard, the commentators—journalists or novelists, movie directors or poets—all realize they must play their records within the system. No wonder, then, that their books, lyrics, plays, and films define the limits as well as the seductive power of America's prevailing mythology. However disturbed by the system, the critics stay cool and fall back on the only available political faith—the Myth of the Liberal Enlightenment, the promptings of Thomas Hobbes and John Locke, the legacy of the Founding Fathers.

And the consumers of criticism remain no less composed as they show their appreciation of their country's troubles. It is as if everyone were enrolled in some art-appreciation course in which the meaning and range of the subject matter had been settled long ago. Readers relax with Norman Mailer:

> The heat in our juvenile delinquency is matched only by the unadmitted acceleration of our race into cancer, that disease which is other than disease, that wave of the undifferentiated function, the orgy of the lost cells.
> So, yes, it may be time to say that the Republic is in real peril. . . .[1] *

*Notes and Sources follow Chapter 9.

Moviegoers find themselves relishing the explosion of household goods which ends Antonioni's "Zabriskie Point." Students of the culture derive stimulation by patronizing Timothy Leary, Don Juan, Lenny Bruce, R. D. Laing, Herbert Marcuse, or whatever guest will surely depart before the discussion gets serious. Yet for producers and consumers of criticism, nothing beyond the fringe promises redemption. None of the alternatives to American liberalism appear sufficiently meaningful to offer *ground* for moving ahead. Ideas or programs which transcend the dominant culture are treated as contributions to what Irving Howe has deplored as "a frolic of emptiness," as a "fate worse than death."[2] To depart from liberalism, so it is made to appear, means the end not only of an authentic America but of the very possibility of civilization. And the vision of *that* catastrophe is sufficient to make the home-grown critics of America hope for a therapeutic home-coming, an old-fashioned uncorrupted politics, a return to the great settlement of 1789. Outside lies madness.

Insofar as this consciousness is the basis of acceptable criticism, the critiques of America serve to disclose the limits of the liberal imagination. Their very style and structure are revealing. Their well-composed metaphors, the sanity of their tone, and the emotions they repress help to clarify what the dominant culture amounts to, which direction it impels Americans to drift, and where it ultimately leaves them stranded.

Because the dissenting critics remain incorporated in the very institutional order they subject to scrutiny, it turns out that they are as frustrated as everyone else who falls within the range of their vision. Like all who have been defeated in suburbs and apartments, supermarkets and legislatures, universities and hospitals, welfare offices and professional associations, the critics are unable to *develop* feasible strategies for self-fulfilling action. They remain but witnesses to the incompleteness of American life. At the same time, they unwittingly reveal what is missing: a community so organized that it will do justice to their unexpressed feelings, that it will allow for second acts in American life. It is true, of course, that such films as "Midnight Cowboy," such documentaries as "An American Family," such journalism as Capote's *In Cold Blood*, and countless novels reveal individuals pathetically out of touch and unrelated. Again and again, the center of American life is shown to be a stage on which people are disconnected, cracking up, and moving aimlessly. But once this observation is made, the critiques come to a dead stop.

It should be evident that there can be no avoiding the dead end of the critics —of Americans generally—until they identify the constraining beliefs that drive them toward despair, silence, and self-annihilation. Failing to raise the Myth of Liberalism to the level of consciousness, they keep returning to it even as they point to America as cancerous, stifling, and one-dimensional. Remaining unexpressed, their amorphous awareness of the time-out-of-joint serves again and again merely to make Americans more bitter, more despairing and ugly, less capable of acting. The way out, clearly, is to make America's mythological props more explicit. It is to expose the ramifications of those lofty abstractions which have become the familiar iconography of liberalism—freedom, individualism, opportunity, competition, enterprise, and achievement. It is to express the present-day *meaning* of the terms which constitute the inarticulate background of the public ceremonies and basic texts of America's culture.

The myth to which Americans keep returning as they sense themselves to be under pressure can be seen in its most explicit form in the writing of its originators—that is, in the political theory of eighteenth-century English liberalism. Determined to defend a new regime in opposition to repressive feudal institutions, Thomas Hobbes, John Locke, Adam Smith, and James Madison were *compelled* to elucidate, and they did so unashamedly. They frankly proclaimed that a society was wanted in which everyone would be committed to the rational pursuit of self interest. They elaborately announced their faith in salvation through private endeavor. Their political program was

---

I have used the example of Ancient Mesopotamia because of its simplicity, because, like the cleaned skeleton of an animal or bird, it displays the obvious. But every literate society which has so far existed has needed to use the past for the same fundamental purpose. The past has always been the handmaid of authority.

—J. H. Plumb

---

derived from the assumption that the pleasures of living are enhanced when the individual distinguishes himself from nature and then forces it to yield its goods. Mastering it, he can employ it for his own pleasure. The price of civilized life is nothing less than nature subdued. In Hobbes's terms, man will live more commodiously and suffer less from nature—including his own—when he takes account of his drive for power and uses his inborn ingenuity to act in his interest. Fortunately, the individual is not only self-aggrandizing and acquisitive but also endowed with reason. True, he is hopelessly self-interested. But he is also able to reflect on his interests. Taking rational account of them, he considers their consequences and minimizes his discomforts.

Hobbes saw the implications of these views without flinching. Man is a creature of insatiable appetites which he is driven to satisfy. Because nature would not freely cater to man's drives, the human economy must be one of scarcity. It follows that individuals necessarily struggle with one another for sheer survival in a hostile world. In crisp phrases, Hobbes noted that in an ungoverned state of nature everyone is at war with everyone else and that "there is no place for industry, because the fruit thereof is uncertain; and consequently . . . no account of time; no arts; no letters, no society and, which is worst of all, continual fear, and danger of violent death; and the life of man, solitary, poor, nasty, brutish, and short." Only by using their power of reason can individuals hope to escape terror and anarchy. They can persuade themselves and one another to submit to the laws of a sovereign, peace-keeping power. That is, men are sufficiently rational to permit some sovereign authority to maintain order and thereby make their lives less nasty, more civil. Thus the agenda of liberalism was set: the individual, not being civil in and by nature, must be *made* civil by governmental institutions and civic education. A governmental structure above him must be empowered to civilize him.

To this vision, John Locke added an appealing democratic ingredient. The way he extended Hobbes's theory made it palatable in a world in which an emerging middle class had questioned the divine rights of kings, attacked feudal institutions, and broken into the political arena. Hobbes had concluded that men needed to be subjected to the virtually unlimited, irrevocable power of civil government. Without denying power to this authority, Locke made it revocable. He claimed it could safely be made dependent on the free consent of the governed. Locke was able to relax and trust an electorate because he believed that free citizens would use their reason not only to calculate their best interests and accept an impersonal constitutional order (as Hobbes had granted) but also to consider what is morally right. They would consult their consciences, reflect on the universal moral law of nature, and then act accordingly.

Because the thinkers of the Enlightenment had no cause to worry about the consequences of freeing rational individuals to pursue their own interests, they could easily plead for freedom. In fact, they argued for the destruction of all political, economic, and religious monopolies, against all publicly supported establishments. They were revolutionaries because they were simply unconcerned about the consequences of private innovation, dynamism, and restlessness. John Locke (who first elaborated on this doctrine), Adam Smith (who related it to man's economic life), and James Madison (who applied it to the New World) were untroubled as they contemplated the public effects of private ambition. None feared that selfish pursuits would destroy the public interest, the general welfare, the common good. In their view, justice *is* the free interplay of private interests—nothing either base or sublime above and beyond that. Because they saw justice *implicit* in the operation of the system, they had no reason to inquire whether public agencies independent of private interests needed to be *explicitly* concerned with justice—or with its absence.

An explicit concern for the community as such could be dispensed with because of three commanding assumptions, each integral to the Liberal Myth.

Given the hostility and potency of nature and man's limited capacity to control it, individuals, it was assumed, can do only so much harm in any case. Moreover, within the limited sphere they occupy, individuals will behave reasonably enough because they are morally governed by what Locke called "right reason." And finally, while individuals would be kept in their place in private life by an intractable nature and their God-given conscience, in public life a well-designed constitutional order could prevent them from becoming

---

. . . confidence is everywhere the parent of despotism—free government is founded in jealousy, and not in confidence; it is jealousy and not confidence which prescribes limited constitutions, to bind down those whom we are obliged to trust with power: that our Constitution has accordingly fixed the limits to which, and no further, our confidence may go. . . .

—Thomas Jefferson

---

overbearing. In short, an autonomous nature, man's innate moral sense, and a political system of institutionalized checks and balances will best provide for the maximum fulfillment of individual interests.

In this ingenious formula, the tasks of government and politics define themselves. The function of government is to protect private initiatives and, of course, to exercise that power which inheres in *any* government—the power to preserve society as a whole. Ideally, government is so constituted that it will automatically respond to unforeseen threats against civil society. The intricate mechanisms of the constitutional order—not impetuous idealists —will handle the exigencies of life. Whether governmental responses to crises come to be labeled "legislative," "executive," or "judicial," they will serve to redress imbalances that occur outside the fixed boundaries of the governmental system. Lest liberty be destroyed, legislation will cope with emergencies as they arise—one at a time, piecemeal, incrementally.

Beyond curbing economic interest groups which forever seek to capture governmental power, public policies will meet all threats to the security of the nation. What conditions are in fact threatening ones is perfectly clear. Depressions, insurrections, wars, natural disasters—occurrences that might justify the full use of governmental resources—will define themselves. Attacks on Fort Sumter, the battleship *Maine*, Pearl Harbor, or Saigon are just as self-evidently dangers to the nation's life as crime, unemployment, inflation, and poverty. The meanings of "war," "riot," "disaster," "energy crisis," "depression," "subversion," "provocation," or "neurosis" are so obvious to reasonable men—so clearly set—that it becomes needless to *justify* governmental responses. Responses are simply *called for*. Situations themselves dictate and validate the proper course of action in prose that virtually writes itself. Public power, in any event, is seen as always extensive enough to meet whatever situation calls for its exercise and, at the same time, as limited by the consensus that defines the situation as an "issue"—that is, as demanding action.

As a result, the range of politics—public action, public life—is *objectively* delimited. Politics is properly kept from interfering with what is presumed closed and settled. Economic, cultural, and spiritual enterprises are expected to remain private matters, not to be publicly debated and changed. An open-ended, permanently unsettling politics is seen as having happily ended with the original adoption of the institutional arrangements of liberalism, the establishment of constitutional government which made it pointless to keep reopening such fundamentals as the nature of welfare, the place of the arts, the character of education, the structure of the family, the meaning of property, the organization of work, or the consequences of privacy. The basic society-wide order—man's unwritten constitution—can at last be regarded as given and venerable. Politics consists not of the perpetual reexamination and

> The danger of disturbing the public tranquility by interesting too strongly the public passions, is a still more serious objection against a frequent reference of constitutional questions to the decision of the whole society. Notwithstanding the success which has attended the revisions of our established forms of government, and which does so much honor to the virtue and intelligence of the people of America, it must be confessed that the experiments are of too ticklish a nature to be unnecessarily multiplied. . . . The decisions which would probably result from such appeals would not answer the purpose of maintaining the constitutional equilibrium of the government.
>
> —James Madison

restructuring of fundamentals but of working within the system—a game promising sufficient excitement for those able to afford playing it.

If the individual enters the politics of liberalism at all—and even by casting a ballot he makes a partial appearance—it is to reap some specific reward, something that, when all goes well, enriches his private life. The point of electioneering, voting, lobbying, and holding public office is to secure some advantage or at least to prevent harm from being done. According to the Myth of Liberalism, the rewards lie not in the process of politics but in some calculable results; the process is merely what one must put up with. Because most candidates and most bills are defeated, frustration is inevitable. Political participation means giving up the joys and pleasures of private life. To occupy public office is to make a sacrifice. Nothing but misery is gained by someone who enters politics to express new interests and integrate them in the

luxuries, industrial statesmen and cultural arbitrators will bring the despoilers of nature or the violators of cultural decorum to their senses. When private sanctions such as blacklisting, contract cancelations, franchise revocations, or denial of access to raw material fail to be effective, agencies of government can be called on to implement the recommended policies. The heads of private groups will enlist school boards, licensing bodies, and regulatory commissions. They will rely on public administrators to enjoin pornography, faulty wiring, negligent medical practices, or most basically to keep unaccredited, unschooled, and unruly outsiders in their place.

Since private power is unequally distributed in the liberal society, the few who exercise a disproportionately large share of it not only determine the limit of what is acceptable within the dominant culture but also seek to neutralize those countercultural impulses which the economy cannot convert into profits. It becomes the duty of representatives of the respectable culture to guard universities, museums, libraries, theaters, and finally the streets against the social dynamism—the uncouthness—generated by efforts of new interest groups to make their appearance. Thus cultural traditions and enduring values are reinforced by servants of power who, while never explicitly defining good taste or clean living, keep reflecting how imperative it is to separate leisure from work, play from reality, culture from politics and, above all, art from life. They write and speak as if these compartments were given by nature and their contents had settled meanings. Relying on the same inarticulate consensus that is believed to define "peace," "prosperity," "leisure," or "delinquency," they proceed to draw the line between necessary and optional tasks. Knowing what is "essential" and "real," they deplore the way some critics speak sarcastically of *so-called* crime or *alleged* insanity as if crime or insanity were fictions. In short, those who have emerged as society's trustees certify for others what is immutably real, what is truly law-abiding and sane, or what is authentic Theater, Music, Literature, Language, or Education.

I realize that the repressive—and uplifting—elitism which I am attributing to liberalism does violence to the complex hopes of eighteenth- and nine-teenth-century liberals. After all, they sought to release man's creative potential and overturn the suffocating religious, economic, and political orders of their day. They wished to deprive elites of the power to dictate the individual's private beliefs and personal conduct. Yet as the force of their revolutionary thrust has been exhausted, they have left a legacy of ideas which today block the emergence of alternative social policies. *An ideology originally designed to vindicate private rights now serves to legitimate the maintenance of the established equilibrium of interests.* The beliefs which sustain constitutionalism serve to guard against the emergence of the very conflict which liberal thinkers from Immanuel Kant to John Stuart Mill saw not as a prelude to order but as good in itself.

The very language of liberalism has led to a definition of "reality" as that which happens to be the status quo. It has become only natural to "let the facts speak for themselves." To be understood, one refers as literally as possible to the reality which is manifestly "out there," a reality so autonomous that it is seen to act on the passive populace by informing and instructing it, by imposing its forms and structures. One's words will ideally conform to the existing order of facts. Things being quite clearly what they are, they can and should be formulated in clear terms. To be authentic, the knowledge provided by history or science will correspond to the way the world has come to be.

By attaching individuals to familiar aspects of reality and alienating them from unknown ones, liberalism protects people not from new experience but from new *expressions* of experience. They can use no fresh ways—no new forms of expression—for coming to terms with it. True, people might still express unrealized alternatives to everyday reality. But such expressions will be perceived as "unrealistic." The espistemology of liberalism makes certain that utopian speculation, religious enthusiasm, and artistic expression are kept disconnected from the "real" world of politics. Public life is thereby meticulously confined to previously accredited dimensions.

Political discourse is couched in language which assumes that the order of things has been completed some time ago. The stress is on remaining true to the original intention of lawmakers, most basically to that the Founding Fathers. To be sure, the language of politics is fluid enough to allow for additional touches to the foundations of public life; the constitution of the liberal state may be freely elaborated. But because the definitions of the basic terms of public conduct are established, no fundamental restructuring is thinkable. There can be no doubts about what it *means* to be reasonable or to be public-spirited, to work and to succeed, to have status, property, integrity, or knowledge. Vocabulary-building means studying the dictionary rather than inventing terms to create new realities. Words are seen not as continuously variable human constructions by which a community of individuals keeps redefining its existence but rather as mirrors for reflecting the preordained pattern of society. As a result, the language of politics—of public life—is depersonalized. The acceptable reason for giving and following instructions is that "it's policy" or that "it's official." Thus power relations are masked from those who give instructions and those who receive them. Both the bureaucrat and his client will accept situations as "logical" when orders are given in impersonal official language. Superiors and subordinates, parents and children, men and women, guards and prisoners, nurses and patients will *know* what is meant when action is prohibited on the ground that "it's not logical" or that "it's not the time and the place for it"—as if some autonomous logic or time or place rather than human convention had dictated proper behavior, as if privileged men had not previously given meaning to the terms of their bargains. Resistance to bureaucratic rhetoric therefore comes to be seen as willful or perverse.

Opposition to directives is quieted by language which is ideally as objective as the "real" world. Explosives become "hardware"; tear gas becomes a "benevolent incapacitor"; a prison becomes a "rehabilitation center." To be sure, incidents such as a riot, a political trial, or a strike may break the pattern of anticipated reality and cause occasional moments of nervousness. The available language, however soothing, may fail to contain emerging turbulence. Yet as the troublesome event recedes, it is assimilated to the familiar structure of experience. The Haymarket riot, the Sacco and Vanzetti trial, or the Vietnam insanity blend with the known and commemorated history of the nation, a history that might seem more fractured were unacknowledged interests included, were more people to participate in its telling.

Thus the past and the present of liberalism are comprehended to the extent that everyone becomes familiar with its officially confirmed elements—or rather with elements confirmed by those who serve to educate the citizenry in the ways of civic responsibility. The basic elements of public life, it is assumed, will speak for themselves. Situations will express their inherent logic; history will tell its own story; facts will be eloquent; statistics will be striking.

And the populace learns to respond. From countless TV programs, journalistic accounts, and college courses, it learns to apprehend and implement "reality." It purchases encyclopedias, absorbs case histories, and uses the latest manuals for fixing existing plumbing, marriages, and political conventions. Books, posters, and songs are expected to function like mirrors and to leave the world intact. Ideally, objective journalism, truth-telling history, and positivistic social science will reiterate the assumptions that define the structure of public life. There may be critics whose odd accents betray their desire to go beyond repairing the system. Yet, as they seek to justify a more comprehensive structure of possibilities, they either have no means for breaking the mirror of the schools and the media—no forms that convey more than the liberal imagination reflects—or else find themselves publicly irrelevant. Serious efforts to cut beneath the surface on which the literal fact meets the camera eye are allowed to assume importance only after working hours. Reportage by Norman Mailer, documentaries by Robert Coles, paintings by Francis Bacon, sculptures by George Segal, or music by Joan Baez are tolerated, but only during time that can be spared. Subversive work moves toward coffee tables, late shows, and middle-class magazines in which it can nestle amidst the ads, serving to stimulate talk about the scandals of the day. At night, the day's excitements become useful entertainments.

Within the epistemology of liberalism, all elements of reality are deemed to be unmistakeably visible, quite clearly *there*. To know them is to accept a truth so plain that it need not be made explicit: the sum total of reality is an aggregation of discrete units rather than an ongoing process which is finally incommensurable. Reality consists of the great abstract entities of modern life, all of them nouns that had been verbs, all of them invisibly capitalized: Worker, Consumer, Product, Commencement, Need, Performance, Decision. Each of these becomes a reified, fixed segment of a once living process. Each becomes a disconnected and self-contained object.

Two sociologists, Richard Sennett and Jonathan Cobb, have noted the social consequences of a belief system which allows one to claim that one knows things only when one can calculate their number and take their measure.

> The pioneering psychologist E. L. Thorndike wondered in books like *Animal Intelligence* (1911) if ability could be expressed in terms of quantity and numbers. He saw that men exercised their intelligence in concrete actions and decisions; they manipulated objects in what were described as intelligent or unintelligent ways. Surely, if one could observe the physical effects of intelligence, one could make a physical measurement of the phenomenon itself. Then one could know "how much" intelligence was needed in the handling of a given situation, or "how much" intelligence a human being possessed. . . . If intelligence can be expressed at all as a tangible commodity, it is evidently like money or stock certificates in other respects as well: it can somehow be increased or lost, earned or squandered.
>
> A fundamental challenge to the idea of intelligence as commodity has been posed by psychologists like Jean Piaget and Barbel Inhelder in Geneva. Intelligence, they say, is rather a process changing over time and place to provide a repertoire of symbols that human beings need to understand their own phases of growth. This view has met a large measure of resistance in this country, for it would rob the psychologist of a peculiar kind of certainty: if he can compute the intelligence of a person, he can know something indelible, something fundamental about that person; in other words a person who is being measured in a test can be classified by it. The system of classification that results causes a few people to stand out as belonging to special classes of high or low, while the great majority are relatively indistinguishable in the middle.
>
> Why should psychologists want to have such knowledge? We might broaden the question, since measures of ability by test and comparison have spread from the school to the office and factory: why is society so curious to know what abilities people have in this comparative and large-scale way? After all, the results can be perverted to destroy a fragile dream, only a few hundred years old, of equality among men.
>
> Ironically, the impulse to determine a person's ability is also the child of the Enlightenment. In eighteenth-century France and England, bright sons of lower-bourgeois families demanded that government and professional positions be opened to persons on the basis of natural ability, rather than of parental influence or hereditary right. . . .
>
> The testing of ability acquires legitimacy in the eyes of its practitioners as the continuation of an old glorification of the individual apart from the social conditions into which he is born.[4]

In the ideal world of liberalism, the individual will be fulfilled insofar as he is distinguished from the mass. When not distinguished, he will feel inadequate. He will strive to finish, to amount to something. If he aspires to less, he feels he is delinquent. Work of his that remains in process he learns to define as a problem to be solved by persistence, diligence, and an increasingly refined division of labor. He expects time-motion studies to fragment the productive process into interchangeable blocks. He knows that time can run out, that it is divisible, and that its parts are worth money. Time can be served and lost and killed. Or when things go badly time can hang on one's hands.

When on occasion Americans have intimations of a more comprehensive world outside the self-contained entities sanctioned by the liberal epistemology, they know such feelings must refer to some unreal inexpressible "otherness" without weight or status. Such feelings must be converted into cal-

---

"Now, of course, the Country Club is being remodeled and it's something of a mess. The old guard there didn't want the changes. They didn't want another cabana. I do not agree with them. I say we must move with the times."

—Kansas City resident

---

culable, measurable units. It becomes rational and therefore imperative to keep reducing whatever experience seems to be more than the sum of its parts, to keep quantifying all the stuff of community and mutual trust, all those incommensurable, threatening things which no one seems to own, which no one can fit into the utilitarian calculus of the liberal culture. Thus pressured, people learn to avoid fluid boundaries, unsurveyed realities, indeterminate contexts, gratuitous action, and the kind of person who goes through life redefining his identity.

The theoretical source for the pressures that lead to a withdrawal from unbounded experience has been identified by Stephen Toulmin, a philosopher who has summed up the epistemology of the eighteenth century:

(1) The order of Nature is fixed and stable, and the Mind of Man acquires intellectual mastery over it by reasoning in accordance with Principles of Understanding that are equally fixed and universal.

(2) Matter is essentially inert, and the active source or inner seat of rational, self-motivated activity is a completely distinct Mind, or Consciousness, within which all the highest mental functions are localized.

(3) Geometrical knowledge provides a comprehensive standard of incorrigible certainty, against which all other claims to knowledge must be judged.[5]

These axiomatic suppositions support the twentieth-century notion that concepts such as time and space, inner and outer, mental and physical, cause and effect, or being and nonbeing refer to basic invariants. Today, being rational means embracing the abstract categories of human knowledge as if they were fixed forever. Reflecting the coherence of the world, these categories are seen as the very constitution of man and nature. They are the undiscussed basis for individual conduct and social policy.

The epistemology of liberalism makes activities appear rational to the extent that they are the appropriate means for reaching a predetermined end. Activities which have no such purpose consequently come to be regarded as disreputable. If idleness and play are nevertheless esteemed, they are so because they restore man for serious work. It is not for the dream that one dreams. Converting every activity into a means to achieve specified ends, individuals become calculating. And believing that whatever they give they no longer have, they learn to ration their resources, not excluding their capacity for affection.

The practical lessons are clear. Commit yourself to some course of action so as to reach a worthy end. Take courses for credit, credits for certification for employment, employment for money, money for a life that

_____

"It figures."

—American expression

_____

makes it possible to watch the next generation repeat the quest for some end result. Expect rewards to be deferred. Your golden years—the ad for retirement plans remains convincing—will come, if it all works out, at the end.

Becoming absorbed by the means to reach ever-receding ends, the individual experiences the whole of reality as unsatisfying. The ends—happiness, normalcy, cleanliness, success—are categories whose unchanging content is self-evident. Fixed categories, they organize work until something breaks down and people feel the dread of being no more than they are. But even then, they may still be consoled by the Liberal Myth: the present is surely but the prelude to a richer future. By remaining industrious during that meantime which stretches before them, men can yet redeem the troublesome present. Deprivations currently experienced can be overcome by courses in self-improvement. Both at home and abroad, educational programs can bring ever more people within the liberal fold. By adhering to the distinction between serious curricular and playful extracurricular activities and by emphasizing fixed subject matter rather than the continuous redefinition of ends in the process of living, schools and other mass media can promote the liberal virtues of rationality, tolerance, and work. Ultimately, the mission of the carriers of the Myth of Liberalism is to overcome pockets of resistance, to transcend national boundaries, to help all mankind experience the blessings of liberty by persuasive example, if possible, and by relying on such international networks as I.T.T. or the World Bank, if necessary. For those with vision, assuredly all is well.

2

The Institutional Frame

Defeated in our most fundamental enterprises, we may find it possible to appreciate Lucretius's vision of a universe in which "the systems and their suns shall go back slowly to the eternal drift," in which "nothing abides" and "all things flow . . . until we know and name them." Weary at the end of an era, we may slowly begin to acknowledge that the world is radically ambiguous, "a monster of energy, without beginning or end" (Nietzsche), an "absurd malady" (Camus), a "meaningless sequence of forces" (Henry Adams, to whom I will return), and that it is we ourselves who stabilize the world by calling things good and evil, goods and evils being merely so called. If the knowledge of inescapable ambiguity can liberate—if it can free us to hold and name things, to redesign man and society—it also imposes responsibilities for which nothing in the Myth of Liberalism equips us.

As Americans seek some footing in the face of the contemporary drift, liberalism offers no help. They become fatigued and apprehensive, and this all the more as they sense not merely the end of the ingenious formula of the eighteenth-century Enlightenment but also the void beyond the officials empowered to implement the formula. And without confidence in one's custodians, managers, teachers, parents, judges, or presidents, how can one keep one's balance? What educational system, what discipline and law, what constitution will contain the fluidities of experience and give direction to one's existence?

Certainly the Myth of Liberalism has become hard to fall back on. Unanticipated consequences of the industrial revolution have made its collapse increasingly evident. The eighteenth-century assumption that nature can be counted on to place limits on man's ambition has been undermined by the forces of technology. Rivers, mountains, and deserts no longer pose barriers to human organization as technology has empowered Americans to consolidate their scattered energies. The biosphere of the planet is at the command

and mercy of privately organized, publicly unaccountable collectivities which the Myth of Liberalism ignores.

There might be less concern about this triumph over nature if only the other elements of the Myth of Liberalism were still intact to provide a basis for personal freedom and self-government. The philosophers of eighteenth-century liberalism relied not only on the barriers to oppression erected by nature but also on those posed by the individual's conscience. They assumed that if you left the individual alone, he would be guided by "right reason"— perhaps bolstered by his family, school, and church. Private authorities would serve to keep everyone virtuous and upright and civil. True to his conscience, the individual would develop his potentialities with due concern for the community, the common good, and one another.

Yet it has become quaint to believe that the moral law which was expected to govern private relations has retained its authority. Americans are restrained only by the limits of their energy as they abuse nature and one another in the pursuit of their private ambitions within a market economy. There would seem to be no moral language for making public policies persuasive; the only generally acceptable criteria for judging the desirability of new objectives are quantitative and technical. The only recognized depression is an economic one, and its only legitimate cure is economic growth by private effort.

Nor can public goals be confidently advanced by governmental agencies: the Myth of Liberalism dictates that governmental bodies be systematically frustrated in their efforts to plan public objectives. Government is to be checked and balanced. Lest it become tyrannical, its power is to be divided geographically and separated functionally. Frustration is built into the system. In the shape James Madison gave to the Myth of Liberalism, the political system was to guarantee that no majority could ever succeed in imposing a policy objectionable to established interests. In the private sector, it is true, the individual would be free to make of himself what he chose. But public government was to be inhibited.

Yet this part of the Myth, too, has been collapsed by the facts. Private government became public long ago. Nationally organized private groups not only make policy which shapes the lives of individuals who work within them but also govern nominal outsiders who have no options. Not subject to political checks, the leadership of corporations, unions, and professional associations pursues objectives that are national and all-embracing. In fact the entire governmental system—private government and public government— has become interlocked. Politically unconstrained minorities govern the populace. Virtually autonomous men in command of industrial and financial empires integrate diverse private interests and enact public policy.

The array of policies which emerge unaffected by the constraints of nature, individual morality, and constitutional mechanisms has left Americans feeling cheated and perplexed. There would seem to be no way out. No image of the past or of the future suggests options. Implicated in the affairs of the day, the individual can find no vantage point for coming to terms with his fate. Everything is exhaustively settled for him, if not by the Myth of Liberalism, then by his life as lived. Although he may sense the presence of a richer reality, he has no access to it. The language available to him for

---

One man on West 85th Street, who sleeps late every morning, always looks out his window before he goes to bed to see if there are any double-parked cars nearby. When he sees one, he calls the police. It does not do much good, he says, but it always makes me feel better.

—*The New York Times*, November 18, 1971

---

exploring alternatives, the language of techniques and numbers, leads but to more of the same. The existing symbols merely reaffirm the familiar surface of his life.

It is not only their language that keeps Americans locked into the established present. The physical settings in which they move through the curves of their days and nights convey the same message: *this* is it, and *that's* all. Implicit in the very flow of merchandise that surrounds Americans is the singular message that the world they know is the only possible world. The existing institutional order seems to exhaust the range of possibilities. The two-party system, the inventory of supermarkets, the curriculum of the schools, the organization of business, and the news filtered by the media are the whole of reality. There is nothing ambiguous, open-ended, or multi-dimensional about white bread, airline terminals, retirement centers, stockholder meetings, medical service, or even travel abroad. All of these elements of modern life are artifacts devoid of irony. Each is so fully and wholesomely present that its mere existence communicates its desirability. When, for example, medicine is so organized as to connect healing to profits—and when doctors are systematically kept in scarce supply—it becomes unthinkable to consider alternatives to the entrepreneurial concept of the doctor: the doctor *is* in business, and that's how it is. When steps lead *up* to city hall or a fence *encloses* the White House, the message is clear. When a highway system replaces an array of footpaths, when houses "come with" washing machines, when classroom chairs are riveted in parallel rows, or when traffic officers are armed with more than whistles, an indubitable reality advertises itself. Alternatives are unknown and not in demand. Other realities—possibilities above or beneath the lives said to belong to Americans—are *ruled* out. There is no time—that great autonomous entity personified by liberalism—for anything else.

Nevertheless, Americans find time to be disconcerted. Shouldn't their institutions, their very language, sustain them more fully? Shouldn't they be able to satisfy their ill-defined need to keep identifying and relating more diverse potentialities? By now, their litany is familiar. Individuals complain they are unseen and unrelated, privatized and deprived, prematurely finished. As they reach their end, they say that it is not *their* end, that something has been left out, never got included in their conversations, diets, marriages, trips, or bargains. They perceive aspects of themselves that might have *remained* unsettled—open to change—but that somehow turned out to have been settled more conclusively than they thought. They have been brought to some dead end which they did not define for themselves. Understandably, they wish to gain a greater measure of detachment from the existing institutional order and perceive it not simply as "the way it is" but as a distinct problem. The world would then *look* different however much it remains the same. Specific parts of it would suddenly become identifiable as hindrances, would appear as crippling and ultimately lethal insofar as they keep individuals from developing themselves and living out their lives. Moreover, once "reality" is treated as problematical, specific private troubles could be traced to a larger setting and thereby become more public and more manageable. It would then be easier to preceive to what extent Americans not merely are quiet and troubled but *are made* quiet and troubled by their environment— the institutional order of liberalism. If, then, I am about to focus on the practices that inhere in America's corporate structure, this is because we can see these not as a solution to the problem of frustrated development but as the problems themselves. They can be seen as keeping masses of people from expressing themselves, from deciding on their own which of their manifold feelings to deaden and which to bring to life.

Under the aegis of the Myth of Liberalism, corporate business has emerged as virtually sovereign in America. Elite-governed industrial and financial giants have become the effective integrators of conflicting interests; they have emerged as the all-absorbing determinants of opportunities for generating options for the whole of society. The results have been gratifying. Competition among a plurality of hierarchies of power is felt to promote justice. Commercial, agricultural, religious, professional, philanthropic, and cultural groups are believed to compete in such a benign way that democracy continues to be served: equitable public policy spontaneously results from their interaction. The old theory of individualism is thereby saved by the new one of group pluralism. Although sovereign groups replace sovereign individuals, the self-regulating process of interest-group competition allegedly makes everything come out well—if not now, at least in the long run.

Against this consoling view, a host of critics have shown that even under the label of pluralism an industrially advanced society cannot deliver what it is said to promise. To base the organization of society on the Liberal Myth means in practice to favor well-endowed groups over whoever has not found his voice. Indeed, it means to make governmental agencies their servant. The leadership of established interests—of men who control groups such as the Chase Manhattan Bank, the Industrial Pollution Control Council, the American Medical Association, or the Farm Bureau—turns out to formulate what in effect is public policy. While the organization's rank and file commutes and works and relaxes, the leadership gauges what might serve the public and determines the level and distribution of national income, directs the allocation of resources, and decides the direction of technological, economic, medical, and educational development. Those who cater to the needs of the corporate state fix the level and the conditions of employment, the structure of wage rates, and the terms, tempo, place, and season of production. The men at the top decide which labor markets and individual skills to use and which ones to reject. They control the quality of goods and services as well as the quantities and standards of consumption. If they cannot induce anyone to buy some specific brand, they can yet make everyone feel

---

"Feminine hygiene is going to be a big business for agencies. Our stuff, Feminque, is selling well. FDS is doing well. Johnson & Johnson came out with Vespre and it's doing well. The American businessman has discovered the vagina and like it's the next thing going. What happened is that the businessman ran out of parts of the body. We had headaches for awhile but we took care of them. The armpit had its moment of glory, and the toes, with their athlete's foot, they had the spotlight, too. We went through wrinkles, we went through diets. Taking skin off, putting skin on. We went through the stomach with acid indigestion and we conquered hemorrhoids. So the businessman sat back and said 'what's left?' And some smart guy said, 'The vagina.' We've zeroed in on it. And this is just the beginning. Today the vagina, tomorrow the world. I mean, there are going to be all sorts of things for the vagina: vitamins, pep pills, flavored douches like Cupid's Quiver (raspberry, orange, jasmine, and champagne). If we can get by with a spray, we can sell anything new. And the spray is selling."

—Advertising executive

---

that automobiles, life insurance, and aspirins are the bases of the good life. As they engage in their diverse operations, corporate organizations assume the burden of leading conflicting interests toward the common good. They embrace—often with sincere tenderness—equity owners, employees, suppliers, distributors, and the mass of free and equal consumers.

Possessing a surplus of material and financial resources, corporations turn from accumulating profits to spending for welfare, making not only narrowly economic decisions but also broadly political ones. Retaining most earnings, management frees itself to engage in philanthropic, aesthetic, educational, and research activities. Thus private men shielded from public control emerge as stewards of the public interest and become political actors. They can see themselves empowered to form a more perfect union, promote the general welfare, and secure the blessing of liberty. They emerge on the public stage, there to define and supply the nation's material, cultural, and spiritual goods. Responding to one another's cues, they effectively govern.

Such government by private interests is reinforced by the liberal notion that decentralizing public government will free people to enter and leave "private," "voluntary" organizations at will. Yet in fact it is only marginally possible to practice one's trade outside the corporate structure. The unaffiliated doctor is as effectively handicapped as the unaffiliated truck driver or farmer. And decentralized government, far from returning "power to the people," actually buttresses power that remains centralized under private auspices. Insofar as associations are actually neither private nor voluntary, their oligarchical structure institutionalizes existing inequalities. Moreover, governmental intervention merely leaves matters where they are. Grants to the currently established system of medical care, for example, simply solidify prevailing inequalities and prevent the emergence of alternatives. As Barbara and John Ehrenreich have shown in *The American Health Empire* (1971), subsidies to patients, hospitals, medical schools, drug companies, and physicians serve to perpetuate a preoccupation with profits. Medical conglomerates connected to private universities are as little interested in giving priority to public health as the automobile industry is devoted to giving priority to pollution-free transportation. Bureaucratic expansion and increased earnings turn out to be the decisive criteria for decision-making.

Depicting the reality behind the Liberal Myth, a multitude of scholars has documented the elite-serving functions of prevailing policies.[1] Their work exposes the deceptiveness of its central dogma that personal freedom is extended when the government disperses funds, acts as a neutral umpire among the powerful, and helps administer the powerless. They reveal the myriad ways in which the corporate state actually restricts authentic participation to the few who administer the rest.

In the liberal scheme, corporate structures are not perceived as political: politics is simply not seen as the business of the economic, seemingly private sector. The economy is nonpolitical by definition. Therefore the individual's right to participate in the public sector is not seen as related to the sector defined as private. It is simply assumed that democratic processes are out of place in the economy: after all, no one is involved in "private" enterprise unless he wishes to be.

The illusion of consensus is even more insidiously maintained when participation, far from being eliminated, is encouraged in all areas except those which define the organization's distribution of power or its given objective. It is not always evident, as Ira Katznelson has noted, that repression is institutionalized:

> Ruler-oriented decentralization programs are often successful in making their system-oriented intent difficult to grasp for two basic reasons. Ruler-initiated decentralization programs *do* increase citizen's opportunities to participate in government in terms both of the numbers of access points and of the directness and immediacy of ruler-subordinate contacts. And, secondly, the nature of their enterprise requires rulers who support and initiate programs of decentralization to clothe their creations in democratic, participatory garb.[2]

During recent years, as organizational blueprints have become increasingly amorphous, they have opened up spaces for the expression of dissent. Everyone would seem to have the chance to participate in making policy. A concern for democratizing bureaucracies appears to have changed the structure of command and obedience and opened the door to change. Yet despite rank-and-file participation nothing changes when everyone defines efficiency in terms of the money cost of an organization's end product. In fact, since it has become evident that people are apt to become even more efficient when they *feel* they participate in the administration of their enterprise, enlightened organizations allow for widely consultative decision-making. Executives have learned to stay loose, and they remark in passing that the new informality actually yields long-term benefits—greater productivity and cheaper end products. They gladly enlarge the calculus of costs and benefits, noting that an atmosphere of equality not only contributes to efficiency but also ties people to their jobs by reducing individual alienation. Payoffs all around, the new cyberneticists rightly observe.

When the ends of private organizations are defined by those in power, not even the most widespread participation in decision-making can have any bearing on the ends. Participation can then serve only to implement what

---

More than a third of the nation's federal income has been spent for more than a generation in order that the congressmen who give the generals the money they ask for will then be re-elected with money given them by the corporations that were awarded federal money by generals who, when they retire, will go to work for those same corporations.

—Gore Vidal

---

those in power believe to be in their interest. Thus, under the banner of economic freedom, private elites are able to govern unconstrained by the constitutional system which checks public government.

The consequent double standard—freedom for the economy, restraint for the polity—might be more blatant if those who have been in command of the economy had all been self-conscious conspirators, or if they had never had philanthropic impulses, or if a steady outpouring of goods had not been made possible by America's natural wealth, or if Horatio Alger's fantasy that any boy can succeed with diligence and good manners had been statistically tested, or if executives had not learned to create an atmosphere of permissiveness within their bureaucracies, or if generations of apologists writing history books, movie scripts, and newspaper editorials had been less resourceful. Moreover, it might be easier to see the potency of the economy and the impotence of the polity if the two were in fact neatly separated. But they mesh, and thereby obscure how the participation and consent of the governed become irrelevant to large sectors of the policy-making process. The electorate is deactivated insofar as politicians come and go while the managers of the military-industrial complex carry on. As Virginia Held has noted, the Department of Defense aligned with defense contractors has so narrowed the discretion of Congress and the President that it effectively legislates. And beyond the Pentagon, she sees more—

a vast managerial bureaucracy for nonmilitary governmental activities, including regulatory agencies which serve the interests regulated more effectively than they do the public, and layers of "professionals" and "civil servants" who increase in various ways the distance between the citizen and the source of the decisions made for and about and upon him.

Perhaps, with respect to both industry and government, *the key relation now is between the managers and the managed.* If that is admitted, a number of traditional conceptions may need to be radically revised.

To tell a citizen who is profoundly dissatisfied with his "political conditions" to go out and work for better candidates may seem not utterly unlike telling a working man profoundly resentful of his working conditions to try to persuade the stockholders to select a new management. Formally, stockholders "control" the corporation, and it might be suggested that to get the corporation's management to change its policies, the worker could organize rallies, circulate petitions, leave literature at appropriate doorsteps, and have students with fresh haircuts present to stockholders (sometimes their fathers) face-to-face the arguments for higher wages. The fact that some stockholders hold many votes and others few, while in the political system we are said to be moving closer to what is called a one-man-one-vote electoral process, does not destroy the analogy, because in the realities of contemporary politics some persons have the means to control any possible candidate or to multiply votes through buying television time, hiring advertising agencies, or employing the services of pollsters and influencers. In any case, as we have seen, winning an election in no way assures a significant change of management policy.

As to influencing government through normal interest-group channels, here again economic factors become salient. Citizen groups can hardly hope to pay lobbyists, finance campaigns, and marshal influence in favor of their policies on a scale comparable to that of the Department of Defense and the industries that received $45 billion from its contracts in fiscal 1970, and countless other billions in advantages and favors. Just as in gaining control of a corporation, gaining favorable political decisions normally requires vast amounts of money or positions already held.[3]

It is true, of course, that the impulse of liberalism is to protect the individual's right to influence the decision-making process. Yet when governmental and nongovernmental management become one, governmental action merely preserves unequally distributed economic privileges. If the economy represses the powerless, the polity follows suit. It is true, of course, that antitrust legislation is enacted, holding companies are regulated, oil production is controlled. But a government responsive to the so-called needs of the economy promotes what nongovernmental elites define as industrial peace, an orderly market, a dependable labor supply, and essential research. No wonder, then, that the exercise of power by the Interstate Commerce Commission will generally please the railroads, that state boards of health and the American Medical Association enjoy symbiotic relations, that the operations of licensing bodies and labor-relations boards are supported by the unions, and that the interest in enlarging the defense budget is shared by Defense Department procurement officers and corporate suppliers of military

---

American ideology possesses neither the language nor the inclination for a critical review of the society's private institutions. Ask the average, well-educated citizen to offer some sustained comments on the role and functioning of corporations such as General Motors and General Electric on his society. Apart from a few commonplaces on automobile safety or defective refrigerator handles, he will have nothing to say. If he is asked to evaluate the performance of the president and executives of United States Steel or Union Carbide, he will have no comment. . . .

—Andrew Hacker

---

equipment. Nor can it be surprising that programs to support the disadvantaged result in support for experts who have acquired proprietary interest in the problem. Bureaucracies organized to fight hunger are more vigorously defended by the food processors and distributors than by the hungry. Federal funds for improving educational opportunities benefit bureaucrats in colleges of education and the merchants of audiovisual equipment rather than enrolled students. Model Cities programs become a bonus for city administrators, not a relief for the poor in slum housing. The range of policy alternatives is determined not by those affected by unemployment compensation, job training, public health, food stamps, or public housing but by those in the seats of power—or more generally by an impersonal system in which basic issues were settled long ago. Thus no one questions whether or not workers should *ever* be employed producing cars, asbestos, napalm, or food additives. The issue is only how individuals who suffer from lung cancer, malnutrition, or car accidents might be given more purchasing power through insurance payments to cover their medical expenses. Or more basically, it is how to keep an industry productive enough to cover dividends, salaries, and wages. Fundamentals being settled, those who govern can be perceived as playing their roles in a manner that is neither despotic nor malevolent. As Alexis de Tocqueville anticipated in 1840, elites are allowed to exercise tutelary power while each of the nonparticipants,

> withdrawn into himself, is almost unaware of the fate of the rest. Mankind, for him, consists in his children and his personal friends. As for the rest of his fellow citizens, they are near enough, but he does not notice them. He touches them, but he feels nothing. He exists in and for himself, and though he may still have a family, one can at least say that he has not got a country.
>
> Over this kind of man stands an immense, protective power which is alone responsible for securing their enjoyment and watching over their fate. That power is absolute, thoughtful of detail, orderly, provident, and gentle. It would resemble parental authority if, father-like, it tried to prepare its charges for a man's life, but on the contrary, it only tries to keep them in perpetual childhood. It likes to see the citizens enjoy themselves, provided that they think of nothing but enjoyment. It gladly works for their happiness but wants to be sole agent and judge thereof. It provides for their security, foresees and supplies their necessities, facilitates their pleasures, manages their principal concerns, directs their industry, makes rules for their testaments, and divides their inheritances. Why should it not entirely relieve them from the trouble of thinking and all the cares of living?
>
> Thus it daily makes the exercise of free choice less useful and rarer, restricts the activity of free will within a narrower compass, and little by little robs each citizen of the proper use of his own faculties.[4]

Perhaps the assumptions of liberalism, in particular the belief in a means-ends separation which allows ends to be fixed by "an immense, protective power," can be seen to sustain the loss of control not only by the mass of citizens but by their rulers as well. At the turn of the century, Henry Adams calmly noted how the energies of technology would inevitably unnerve and extinguish the whole of the human species. Making the dynamo the central symbol and the commanding force of modernity, Adams prophesied that an increasingly autonomous industrial state would emerge to transcend all known boundaries. It would imperturbably enforce the law of entropy. Indifferent to the distinction between the managers and the managed, it would grind down the earth and its inhabitants. Adams's pessimism was to be gradually absorbed by popular literature, ultimately by anthologies that share

Power leaped from every atom, and enough of it to supply the stellar universe showed itself running to waste at every pore of matter. Man could no longer hold it off. Forces grasped his wrists and flung him about as though he had hold of a live wire or a runaway automobile. . . .

—Henry Adams

a table of contents so chic, abstract, and commonplace that it could become a substitute for all argument:

     I. Standardization and Routinization
    II. The Unity of Welfare and Warfare
   III. Industrialization and Urbanization
   IV. Bureaucratization and Alienation
    V. The Triumph of Technology
   VI. Terminal Man

Because these phrases have worn thin, we may fail to see their point: behind the disconnected bits and pieces of contemporary technology a unified whole governs. A self-generating and self-serving system, not yet visible, imperiously computes and allocates what is useful, necessary, rational, efficient, and progressive. Permeating society, this system absorbs self-assertive individuals who may emerge on its fringes. True only to its own momentum, it operates as if all problems were solved by continuous production, increasing consumption of natural resources, a steady inflation of goods and services, and the reduction of individual sensibilities.

The feeling of impotence due to a technology which controls the lives of individuals is not alleviated by the prevailing order of America's social institutions. Conventional ceremonies and rituals which ideally serve to *relate* individuals to their fate and to give meaning to their troubles actually fail to provide reassurance at critical moments. As men and women are steered through their lives—through schools, marriages, careers, avocations, hospitals, middle age, and retirement—they are worn out not so much by dramatic disasters as by indiscernible, minute disappointments. Parents left by their children, spouses deserted by one another, or individuals freed from their jobs are no more at loose ends than those who actually find new shelters. Resorts, churches, libraries, summer camps, hobby clubs, communes, colleges, museums, or retirement centers promise personal growth and deliver alienation. Designed to facilitate transitions between the stages of life, admissions offices and induction centers process individuals without reducing their anxieties. People are deadened or made cynical by family life, office procedures, athletic events, graduation exercises, and funeral rites. What is best in people—their capacity for relating—is unused and its lack is unmourned. Traveling abroad in the 1960s, Charles Newman, an editor and writer, recalled a friend who was right particularly on one count—"that our

---

President Nixon has recently boasted that he is the first president in our history who has never missed one day of work through illness, and that he has not even had one headache in his life. It has also been revealed that his weight has not changed in twenty years: that he has recently rendered his austere lunch of rye-krisp and cottage cheese even more spartan by giving up ketchup; and his sole sport, since he has given up bowling and golf, consists of the solitary exercise of running 200 paces in his bedroom in the same spot.

—Francine du Plessix Gray

---

society was not sick because it could be blamed for making him what he was, but rather because it could not make use of what he had made of himself."[5]

The disconnectedness and frustration of individuals flow naturally enough from the hostility to community which liberalism does nothing to deflect. Making a fetish of privacy and of achieving on one's own, liberalism puts all shared activities in jeopardy. It directs men away from common ground and from public affairs, and finally from *every* relationship. People find themselves prematurely ready to quit altogether. Not only the old but all who sense that they have been growing up absurd become listless and soft. The lassitude which is unavoidable for the old, for people who have become exhausted because they have truly employed themselves, becomes an example and a standard for the young: Do no more than you must to feed and

---

In large modern states like our own (if not in others), the individual who feels that he does not matter is the rational man. . . .

—Wilson Carey McWilliams

---

dress and shelter yourself. Let small gestures suffice. Acquiesce, for there is no ground for effective action. Relax. Cool it.

Failing to identify a common basis on which the individual can act in relation to others, the Myth of Liberalism either leaves his capacity for action underdeveloped or else drives him to redouble his efforts. Convinced that

surely there *must* be some payoff, he resents whoever disagrees and quits.
Expected to become self-reliant, he is driven to make himself independent

---

*Fred Gorman, a television repairman, yields to no one in his dislike
of "lazy" people on welfare. Yet his anger is equally great toward two of
his fellow workers who are graduate engineers, but could not survive the
late-sixties depression in the aerospace industry. (Precipitous declines
like this occur, on one account or another, to about thirteen per cent of
professional workers.) Why does a fall from respectability so rare as this
earn Gorman's scorn?*

*"I just don't like people like them among us," he says. "I mean, they
got education." By ideals of personal independence to which he holds,
educated men should not be changing TV tubes. He has become recon-
ciled in his own way to his own position—"I just hack around"—but it is
hard for him to accept the idea that the social order could sacrifice such
men as these. Educated men are supposed, after all, to have an inner,
inalienable freedom, to have developed within themselves the kind of
power no one else can take away. If even they prove weak, it means there
is no security, no freedom, no possibility of escape for himself or for his
children; it means his sacrifices are empty of their meaning. Thus he
rebels at any interpretation of these men's fate which implies that they
were not in control, and insists that they must have perversely decided to
"hack around," troubling men like himself and making them feel afraid.
To have such men as co-workers, then, appears to Gorman not only as a
travesty of the social order, but as a personal insult. Their decline to
equality with him is a kind of betrayal.*

*The anger many workers feel toward students springs in part from the
same root. A refusal to sit on the throne of ability and privilege appears
as a personal insult to those who are denied this seat. If a privileged kid
doesn't want to stay respectable, how can I believe there is any escape
from my own privations? They embody the future and the future is
betraying me.*

—Richard Sennett and Jonathan Cobb

---

from others—even though those "others" long ago ceased to be some overbearing royal establishment, mercantilist economy, or religious hierarchy. He
remains poised to repudiate the community, including the very companion-
ship he secretly craves. Though moving frantically in search of others, he
purchases *self*-help manuals and cherishes his *own* car, house, TV set,
washing machine, and liquor cabinet. He is primed to remain a possessive
consumer by a myth that makes prosperity depend on the pursuit of his private
interests and that defines his happiness as successful repression of his need to
relate.

In sum, the institutional order of the liberal state fails to respond to man's communal needs. Its public policies and social rituals leave people estranged from themselves and one another. Their immediate environment remains incomprehensible to them. Who really can comprehend the supposedly graduated income tax, the research priorities of drug companies, the admissions practices of medical schools, the results of space exploration, or the ingredients added to make milk more wholesome? Payoffs to the poor, to women, and to children—and to men at the top presumably in control of their lives—remain unappreciated. The dominant ideology seems unpersuasive, empty, pathetic. The language is hollow: free enterprise, due process, individual initiative, public service, voluntary association, equal opportunity, happy marriage, constitutional government, defense department, continuing education, creative leisure, guidance counselor, ecological balance, living room, golden years. *None of the adjectives fit.* Once effective and telling, these slogans have ceased to account for the boredom that comes either from being dissatisfied or from having one's dreams realized. Success turns sour—and somehow failure becomes sweet as people incongruously feel good when embarking on a career of rejecting loyalty, of *not* making money, *not* accumulating possessions, *not* speaking clearly, or *not* serving their country.

It is hard to remain tranquil when the very policies that would seem to embody the American dream—policies ensuring clean neighborhoods, fair trials, interstate highways, and mortgage-interest tax deductions—are far from equitable in their impact. As Americans feel the limits of the little myths that bestow legitimacy on their ambitions, the policies that govern their lives lose in authority.

So far, the Myth of Liberalism has made it possible to assume that conflicts generated by the gap between dream and experience could be solved by technicians. Ordinary citizens, except when doing military service, needed only to attend the church of their choice and mind their own business. Crises that might have made the implicit ideology explicit and that might have generated ideological conflict could be deemed amenable to effective treatment—cautious legislation, selective law enforcement, cost-benefit analysis, and high-school social studies. All that remained necessary would be for Americans to urge one another to act in good faith, to get along by going along, to be reasonable and realistic. In the name of political "realism," they could believe that their life would be fulfilling not on common ground on which the individual might give up his merely private enterprises but within a system impelling everyone to compete for the power to live his own separate life as he saw fit.

The outbursts of the 1960s momentarily undermined precisely this "realism." Somehow the unambiguous terminology of law, engineering, war, and accounting failed to do justice to the idealistic passion with which guards shot prisoners, assassins murdered political figures, police pursued hippies, candidates for office sabotaged the opposition, National Guard volunteers killed students, U.S. marshals kept the peace, and military commanders ordered bombings. Nor could the dispassionate terminology of power—presumably the key to individual action—do honor to the intentions of dissident lawyers, doctors, architects, or sociologists. The turbulence of the 1960s could be comprehended even less in terms of economic motives: too many on the Left and the Right were actually working on their own unpaid-for time to clean up the country. It all seemed to be an incongruous situation unexplained by references to economic deprivation. Unaccountably, the American dream of man's universal need to pursue merely private pleasures was in trouble.

Yet despite altruistic outbursts, the mass media, including the schools, continued as before to refer to the dominant order as the whole of the national dream. They kept limiting public options by authoritatively *defining* what is properly political, consumable, sexy, or deserving of military aid. The explosive actions on the margin continued to be diagnosed in time-honored terms as irresponsible but correctable disruptions, as merely private reflexes. America was, in the persisting assumption, one nation under one God, indivisible, with liberty and justice for all. The countercultural movements of the 1960s, like the Nixon presidency, were all mere aberrations. There would surely be an infinity of centennials to acknowledge forever that when everything was finally said and done, America would be not promises but fulfillment.

Given the peculiarities of contemporary life and the limitations of the available mythology, it is understandable that Americans feel troubled. They are continually confronted by phenomena they know are present and nevertheless should not be: *gratuitous* displays of compassion, *unwarranted* bestialities, *useless* self-destructive gestures, *unaccountable* acts of generosity. People have experiences which neither the past as recorded nor the

---

Some began to cry, and others turned to me with betrayed or angry faces, for they had broken free and now there was no way to express what they had done within the rituals of their given world.

—Peter Marin

---

future as expected takes into account: the National Guard at Kent State, Apache braves resisting and then being hanged, Attica under siege, Nat Turner revolting and dying, the Presidency betrayed. Americans are exposed to incredibly depraved and incredibly noble acts. They read about individuals who inexplicably make careers of treason and perversity. They *see*, but cannot articulate what falls in the range of their vision.

Because nothing gives form to the full range of their perceptions, Americans give disproportionate weight to the forms which are available. They mistake the most superficial of negotiations for efforts to resolve fundamental conflicts. They believe that after-dinner parties, union meetings, or political conventions deal with more than trivia. They assume that holidays, elections, or stockholder meetings cut deep enough to matter. Thus they keep public life orderly even while beneath them an offended nature is avenging itself, pushing them out of control, inducing convulsion and delirium. Distraught and apprehensive, they long for surprise-free futures and matter-of-fact communication—anything which promises to reunite private experience and public language.

Unexpressed and unshared life is bound to be experienced as inane—if it can be regarded as experienced at all. Since pains and pleasures persist and yet fail to speak for themselves, people feel themselves in motion, but in motion without context or meaning. Occupying a wild, ungoverned zone without signposts or landmarks, they become bewildered and unnerved. Left speechless, they are at the end of their wits. They become either apathetic or hysterical and yearn for an indiscriminate greening or bloodying—but nothing which mediates, which relates their unidentified interest.

Today, it is clear, the Myth of Liberalism fails to recognize those unacknowledged human interests that continue to emerge unprompted as if determined to perform on their own. The rituals, politics, and language of liberalism take no account of a world beneath America which keeps seeping into its legislatures, organizations, assemblies, courts, conventions, and living rooms. The thin layer of experiences which the Liberal Myth does comprehend—experiences easily converted into numbers, transferred into balance sheets, and deposited in data banks—is bloodless and boring. The very language that is the legacy of an enlightened liberalism has ceased to serve. The Myth is exhausted, bankrupt, useless. It won't work, won't put things together.

3

The Search for a Workable Myth

In the summer of 1971, Vatican authorities posted a nun, Sister Fiorella, at the doors of St. Peter's Basilica to turn away female tourists whose attire was deemed improper. It was hoped she would not be subject to the abuse and assaults of the two men she replaced. Within two months she collapsed—a casualty, the Holy See announced, of "nervous depression"—to be replaced by a novice nun. Officers of the law, gatekeepers, magistrates, guards, custodians, grammarians, censors, and executioners have always been easy to replace (in the Warsaw ghetto of the 1940s, there was no shortage of Jewish police willing to round up Jews). Yet I remain hopeful, for of late the replacements have become disconcertingly unreliable. Many perform their duties beset by doubts. I, myself, wonder if I should not equivocate more and claim less. In this nervous and self-conscious mood, I resemble other authorities who administer educational, military, medical, and economic policies. And as administrators show the strains of having second thoughts, their clientele—mine as well—displays a new measure of self-confidence, refusing to be consoled by announcements that it is being instructed by experts and authors who are unsure about their own message.

Between command and compliance, I am glad to note, there is considerable leakage. A good deal of human energy previously available for maintaining the established pyramids of power has dissipated. The top is not altogether of one mind, the middle not wholly committed to administer what is assumed to be just, and the bottom neither diligent nor compliant. Moreover, dissenters throughout the systems of power are being handled with unaccustomed charity. Prestigious spokesmen have emerged for groups which are subjected to prison rehabilitation, racist policies, slum surroundings, male chauvinism, adulterated food, or inane television programs. New voices are heard if not always heeded. Noblesse oblige. The disaffected are appreciated for displaying wholesome traits that promise renewal of the culture; they are felt to offer a new consciousness, a new ground for being. Their very irrationality—their alleged naturalness and spontaneity—is seen as a token of their worth.

While deploring the decline of authority, men in easy command of the culture—men whose very practices define rationality—are wavering. Inclined toward permissiveness, they are unsure of themselves and their achievements.

One should not cynically underestimate what we can loosely call public spirit. All upper classes profess to act in the public spirit. They are generally successful only so long as by and large their members believe in their job and feel that their privileges do have solid justification. When this confidence wanes, a ruling class is generally finished.

—Barrington Moore, Jr.

They no longer count on their dreams working out. They do not quite trust pharmaceutical research, gasoline mileage claims, police reports, the operations of the F.B.I., the wisdom of the medical profession, or the integrity of the military. Fireproof toys go up in flames.

At home and abroad there is a reluctance to contribute one's energy to governmental enterprises and industrial production. Those in position of power in America vaguely feel—as Lyndon Johnson did just before he resigned himself to not persisting in office—that they no longer have the capacity to work their will in foreign and domestic affairs. Elites may have the raw power—but no compelling ideology to justify its exercise. Unable to articulate persuasive objectives, they cannot confidently present themselves as custodians of the public interest. Doubting the sources of their own authority, they employ image makers, speech coaches, and make-up artists.

In France the kings have always been the most active and the most constant of levellers. When they were strong and ambitious they spared no pains to raise the people to the levels of the nobles; when they were temperate and feeble, they allowed the people to rise above themselves. Some assisted democracy by their talents, others by their vices.

—Alexis de Tocqueville

The prevailing strains are understandable enough. Committed to the maintenance of a law-abiding society, the powerful find themselves recurrently outside the law. They order mass arrests, engage in wiretapping, fail to report taxable income, leak information said to endanger national security, or order the processing of refugees outside the immigration statutes. Even when moving comfortably within the circle of authority, they are troubled as they vote for missiles and highways, redesign neighborhoods, transplant organs, subsidize failing industries, transform the landscape, regiment students, administer the poor, or fix prices. They cannot be quite believed, and know it. Not ever meaning exactly what they say and do, they are dismayed. Transgressors all, they know themselves to be their own enemies.

My hope, of course, is that we can seize the opportunity provided by America's prevailing doubts and hesitancies. The present would seem an ideal time to promote practices which would enable individuals to *remain* of two minds, *continuously* ambivalent toward their achievements and prepared to live with their mixed, contradictory feeling. Not wholly committed to their professed objectives, they should find it possible to follow their intuitions and travel toward those dark, wild regions where men are free from the dominant rationality.

Intellectuals are poor guides for such a trip. "Professors," Philip Rieff has rightly noted, "do not renew a culture. The sources of renewal are no less irrational than the sources of revolutionary death sentences against it."[1] New forms of irrationality—new structures—tend to be conceived in the wilderness among at least half-bewildered figures. Yet I would turn for help to whoever strains, as I do, to call attention to the gaps within both the culture and himself, to unperceived anomalies and fevers, to the sickness of the well-formed body politic—that is, to the very source of recovery. Such efforts may yet become redemptive in a society which, like the American, provides few tribunals for redemption—no viable institutions legitimating doubt, amnesty, weakness, or surrender, no words for people who knowingly squander their talents, who yield and get lost, who decline to be employed, who refuse to shape up, speak clearly, or meet deadlines, who reduce one another's

---

The rich opportunities for redemption which were provided by classical society are gone: no more laying on of hands, no saturnalian release through orgy and role reversal, no cancellation of debts, and above all, no day of atonement.

—Roger W. Smith

---

loneliness without insisting on anything to show for it, who move into a world without either landmarks or monuments, no longer craving to leave records, traces, or scars.

I do not want to be misunderstood as praying for an apocalypse of indolence and negligence. I am pleading for no utopian end of all time—only for the end of time as reckoned by historians who are still attached to "real" heroes, absorbed by "real" decisions, and in search of "real" lessons. Nor am I defending a world of flux without meaning. After all, if we wholly deflate all men and institutions, the end would be but the beginning of new banalities. We would inaugurate a dull and parched society, its renewal literally unthinkable. Accordingly, I would still have us look at ourselves, give the present moment a name and sound its limits.

To give the present moment a name and sound its limits, we perennially search for progenitors and myths. We encourage historians, poets, priests, prophets, and even social scientists to vindicate some genealogy, to give us the word, to reassure us about the *order* of our existence. We want to be told how we happen to be here, why it hurts, why we can't get out, why we should endure. We want creation myths—compact accounts of experiences that strike us as inexplicable.

Americans have recurrently searched for images that might relate (in both senses of the term) the unrelated events of their lives. Struggling to get or keep power, Americans have organized and comforted one another under the banner of such inspiring mythological abstractions as Democracy, New Frontier, Free World, Private Property, Inevitable Progess, National Honor, Manifest Destiny, Free Enterprise, Gross National Product, Individual Initiative, Puritan Ethic, Senior Citizens, and Black Power. Such myths have provided Americans with refurbished pasts and promising futures.

Although there has been no shortage of deliberately created myths to sell candidates, frame issues, and create new life styles, American efforts to mobilize one another have remained amateurish alongside the symbol-mongering enterprises of the totalitarian dictatorships of the present century. Experts in ritual and redemption, European dictators energetically manufactured history to accord with some mythological order. They used all the resources of the state to produce usable pasts, and they had the power to ensure that what failed to conform would be purged and forgotten. In fact, during the first half of this century their manipulation of public opinion was so intensive that it inspired an equally intensive reaction among European intellectuals. Unlike Americans who had taken the perniciousness of myths for granted and never believed themselves to be committed to anything other than honest-to-God truth, European intellectuals were provoked to argue against myth. It was imperative, they said, to make one's way free from illusion or ideology. The most noble of lies, they knew, turn men to ashes. Wherefore European writers, reacting to how their continent had just been ravaged under the cover of ideological crusades, felt the need to proclaim

*The new political myths do not grow up freely; they are not wild fruits of
an exuberant imagination. They are artificial things fabricated by very
skillful and cunning artisans. It has been reserved for the twentieth
century, our own great technical age, to develop a new technique of
myth. Henceforth, myths can be manufactured in the same sense and
according to the methods as any other modern weapon—as machine
guns or airplanes.*

—Ernst Cassirer

what in America was simply taken for granted. Their call for plain common
sense was the American attitude made explicit.

Thus after the Second World War, Americans readily embraced Albert
Camus's anti-ideological stand. Convinced of the *natural* justice of their
politics and the self-evident rightness of their day-to-day practices, Americans found Camus expressing what they wanted to hear. It was equally easy
to acclaim George Orwell for relying on nothing but man's gritty, plain
honesty. As Orwell saw it, men must do their job, whether it is fighting or
writing, without fuss, deception, or heroics. Once clear-minded, they will see
things as they really are. Trust experience and what Orwell called innate
decency. The English philosopher Michael Oakeshott, in another variant of
this view, insisted on the need for straightforward affection for history and
tradition: it was dangerous, according to him, to be oriented by abstract

Rieux rose. He suddenly appeared very tired.
*". . . there's no question of heroism in all this. It's a matter of
common decency. That's an idea which may make some people smile,
but the only means of fighting a plague is—common decency."*
*"What do you mean by 'common decency'?" Rambert's tone was
grave.*
*"I don't know what it means for other people. But in my case I know
that it consists in doing my job."*

—Albert Camus

schemes divorced from "reality." Similarly, the hero of Malraux's *Man's
Fate* could be appreciated in America because, though a Communist, he
dispensed with ideology when he gave his comrade the cyanide that would
have made the end of his own life less horrible: the condemned man re-
sponded not to the dictates of the Myth of Communism but to his own
inarticulate humanity.

Shortly after the Second World War, Ernst Cassirer added scholarly weight to this vision in his *Myth of the State*. Reviewing the injustices rationalized by what he called the magical use of language, he distinguished between semantic language which referred to things as they were and manipulative language which the powerful used as a weapon to produce desired effects. It was time to transcend mythology and restore the semantic function of language. It was imperative not to lie.

The lesson was easy to welcome in America. Speaking the truth—nothing less—seemed to be no trouble when one believed that the gap between ideals and reality was negligible anyway. What need was there to lie when all was patently going well and the New Jerusalem had virtually been built? Skeptics could be assured that one's children at least would be free from drudgery or that, in any case, ideological conflict would come to an end in the post-industrial society. Those who were loyal could discern America even in deviations from its vital center. Given half a chance, the system would work in perpetuity.

Until the 1960s, American historians had little difficulty integrating Indians, indentured immigrants, slaves, populists, suffragettes, strikers, pacifists, reds, and other potential revolutionaries in what was *known* to be a viable culture. Depressions, wars, massacres, lynchings, riots, assassinations, and other interruptions to quadrennial presidential campaigns could be defined as annoying symptoms of mismanagement. To *tell* the story was enough, provided it was honestly told. There was no point in treating the structure of society itself as anything but axiomatically given and as exhausting the range of possibilities. The structure was *all right*: what was recognized as "America" basically encompassed all aspects of the New World's experience. Since interpretation and fact were essentially the same, judgments were dispensable. One merely had to hold the mirror up to society and faithfully attend to the image: it needed no apology. Max Lerner unwittingly illustrated the point in the 1950s in his *America as a Civilization*, a relaxed tour through the landscape, a generous trip without beginning or end, over a thousand pages long, including an acknowledgement to hundreds of collaborators and a massive bibliography for those not fatigued by the excursion. Skeptics had only to engage in further reading; the Book-of-the Month Club and adult education could give everyone his fill.

Yet the belief that the truth would be known if one only committed oneself to endless talk about "the way things really are" turned out to be shaken in the 1960s when events jarred the prevailing image of reality. Above all, the official version of America's role in Vietnam failed to fit the current conception of the nation as self-evidently virtuous. When the constitutional as well as the social system emerged as less than wholly coherent and believable, a new generation of doubters began to search for its voice. It became

Benedict Arnold, Aaron Burr, Axis Sally, William Quantrill, Richard Speck, Leopold and Loeb, Charles Starkweather, Charles Whitman, John Wilkes Booth, Sirhan Sirhan, James Earl Ray, William A. Boyle, Arthur Bremer, Charles Guiteau, Lee Harvey Oswald, Robert Vesco, Bernard Cornfeld, Jay Gould, Al Capone, Machine Gun Kelly, Dutch Schultz, Pretty Boy Floyd, John Dillinger, Frank Costello, Jesse James, Ma Barker, James Michael Curley, Boss Tweed, Edward Hull Crump, Thomas Pendergast, Carmine De Sapio, Bull Connor, Huey Long, Joe McCarthy, Senator Bilbo, George Lincoln Rockwell, G. Gordon Liddy, E. Howard Hunt, Donald Segretti, Egil Krogh Jr., Herbert Kalmbach, Jeb Magruder, John Dean, Frederick LaRue, Dwight Chapin, Billie Sol Estes, Bobby Baker, Spiro T. Agnew, Richard M. Nixon...

But Names Will Never Hurt Us.

On The Bicentennial Of The United States Of America

—*Esquire*, September 1974

thinkable that various fictions were leading (or conceivably misleading) the mass of Americans. The stories Americans told themselves, the holidays they celebrated, even the elections they conducted seemed irrelevant to some larger whole—a truly satisfying life—and this larger possibility had remained unacknowledged by one's parents, teachers, ministers, and politicians. If those in authority were not speaking the whole truth, what was said was a rather special version of it, organizing life in a *partisan* way.

As during every troublesome period in American life, critics began to characterize the dominant myth as being precisely that, not a belief system serving everyone alike. Quite a few Americans, it was remembered, had not landed at Plymouth and were parties to no compact, no peace treaty, no negotiation. No wonder some the magic went out of holidays and flag salutes. It was hard to naturalize Caryl Chessman, Lee Harvey Oswald, Eldridge Cleaver, William Calley, Angela Davis, Spiro Agnew, the Fathers Berrigan, Richard Nixon, Betty Friedan, and Patricia Hearst. It was hard to include Indians, Hawaiians, Eskimos, blacks, Chicanos, or women merely by recounting the so-called facts. References to happiness, justice, welfare, peace, honor, independence, and domestic tranquillity scarcely consoled the defeated and legitimized the victorious. More basically, the mirror held up to society failed to reveal what was central and what was marginal. Had the powerful not emerged as impotent and the wealthy as impoverished?

But whatever the dislocations of present-day America, no effective countervailing myth has emerged to achieve a new integration. The political and moral philosophy of the eighteenth-century liberal enlightenment remains the only general formula for orienting a society in which men have allowed a steadily expanding technology to consolidate individual enterprise, standardize consumption, fix social aspirations, and determine individual roles. Both John Rawls's *Theory of Justice* (1971) and Robert Nozick's *Anarchy, State, and Utopia* (1974) have served to remind Americans how even the most resourceful defenses of liberalism keep them locked into the status quo. Neither the Right nor the Left provides a commanding alternative vision. Liberalism is under pressure, it is true, but less by ideas than by events.

The futility of the search for ideas within the glossary of liberal concepts has led many of the disaffected out of politics altogether. Yet others not so easily defeated have kept on arguing for a return to the incontrovertible fundamentals of America. After all, had not Nature revealed some time ago how Americans ought to organize their lives? If things went badly one only had to appeal all the more strenuously to the nonpartisan truth which could be seen as the *real* America. Assuming the essential soundness of the liberal doctrine, critics merely wanted it implemented more consistently. The

I.C.C., the F.B.I., and the military must be made responsible to Congress.
The poor must be given low-interest mortgages, the young better employment
opportunities, the old better medical care, and everyone a healthier environ-

---

*Certain experiences cannot be formulated because they have oc-
curred too soon. This happens when an inherited world-view is unable to
contain or resolve certain emotions or intuitions which have been
provoked by a new situation or an extremity of experience unforeseen by
that world-view. "Mysteries" grow within or around the ideological
system. Eventually these mysteries destroy it by providing the basis for a
new world-view. Medieval witchcraft, for example, may be seen in this
light.*

—John Berger

---

ment. The litany has become familiar. Release women from housework.
Elect peace-loving congressmen. Respect due process and Ralph Nader.
Break up trusts and restore the competitive market. Change the priorities of
American politics. What is required is good sense and honest leadership.
Formulating no countervailing political theory, legions of critics have been
compulsively returning to that great liberal consensus which John Locke had
given its theoretical basis in the eighteenth century.

The basic textbooks of American politics, government, and history are a
ready-made index to the liberal consensus. Even as their authors, pained by
the dislocations of contemporary America, seek to transcend liberalism, they

---

"Get a hold of yourself."

—American colloquialism

---

retreat to the constitutional framework. Sincere and "concerned," truly
affected by the broken promise of American politics, historians and political
scientists such as James MacGregor Burns, Duane Lockard, and Theodore
Lowi (I am citing but the most fluent) give students the word about America's
troubles. Yet while critical of current public policies, none of these writers
question the ideas which make disaster the norm. They are alert to trouble and
personally upset by it. They point to the red thread of violence, racism,
lawlessness, repression, chauvinism, xenophobia, and genocide which runs
through America. They raise the most radical of questions. And yet they
draw on the old liberal iconography for responses, smoothly pleading for

"equality in freedom," "responsible government," "community control," "juridical democracy," "freedom of the press," "popular sovereignty," "an independent civil service," "a responsible two-party system." To be radical, they know, means to go to the roots. But for them the roots turn out to be politics as usual. They start and end with a wisdom not distinguishable from that of the Founding Fathers.

One useful illustration of an analysis responsive to an admitted crisis in the form that reaffirms its very basis is Duane Lockard's *The Perverted Priorities of American Politics* (1971). It testifies both to its author's perception of disorder and to his resolve to deal with it by going back to what in intro-

---

The remedy is the same as in 1776 and 1787—to rediscover our overarching values, to recommit ourselves to them, to restructure our institutions to fulfill them, and to support and sustain leaders who will serve them. Who will emerge as the Franklin, Washington, Jefferson, Adams, or Madison of our time?

—James MacGregor Burns

---

ductory political-science courses is called the Fundamentals of American Government. He knows all about racism, militarism, imperialism, and poverty. Morever, he is disconcerted not only by these conditions but also by a policy-making apparatus so designed that it produces them as a matter of course. Yet he can merely conclude that America's priorities, not its fundamental structure, are perverted. He establishes no point of view that includes his generous sympathies. He exhibits snapshots of current events but has no words for their larger context, their inner meaning, or the ground against which they might come into relief. For Lockard there is no way for giving expression to the political forces which remain repressed or in repose. He is as enclosed as the political scene he describes. Like other Americans, he can give no focus to his indignation. Failing to relate the conditions he describes to some larger structure of possibilities, failing to fuse the so-called facts with some theoretical ideal, he dissipates his energies. He traverses familiar territory, arrives at the edge, and is at a loss for words.

The case is the same for Theodore Lowi's *End of Liberalism* (1969). Like Lockard, he knows that a radical sounding out is needed. The American republic has lost its legitimacy. In fact, Lowi insists that "the entire *modus operandi* of power must be called into question." His argument is persuasive: a government based on what he calls interest-group liberalism inevitably produces injustice. Public needs are not met. The government's power, though massive, is delegated and ultimately exhausted while private power is enhanced. Policy objectives not formulated at the center of government are ambiguously defined at the margins of the administrative process. Exploiting the prevailing ambiguity, private groups make public law. But what is to be done? Lowi summons the nation to return to traditional constitutional principles.

It is hard to fault political scientists for their conservatism. To what theory, after all, can they appeal? "Lenin arise! They have gone mad!" students sprayed on the walls of the buildings of central Prague in 1968 when interrogators and judges were arrested only to be interrogated and judged in turn. But what can Americans proclaim when outraged by public policies? What patron can they summon? How meaningful is an appeal to Madison? Or to Washington? To which father, which authority, can they turn? What words —what dialectic—can put the entire *modus operandi* of power into question? Locked into America's inarticulate consensus, they have no ground for expanding our knowledge of political possibilities and breaking the boundaries of contemporary public life.

No doubt political scientists occupy a moral vantage point allowing them to see a reality which simply "should not be," which defies the bounds of reason. Yet however troubled by this perception, they do not venture to theorize. They secure no ground for moving beyond the scandals of the day toward a structure within which even *un*reasonable interests might be integrated and redeemed. Immersed in immediacy, political scientists offer little but cases and data, express their dismay, and append their stillborn prescriptions. At most, they evoke sympathy for that part of the populace which finds no legitimate outlets for keeping its spirits up—no courts of appeal, no representatives, no publishers.

The readiness with which the limits of professional political science continue to be accepted as the limits of analysis helps clarify, I think, how hard it is to escape the prevailing rationality. We may sense the need for models to comprehend political life below the familiar surface and to locate reservoirs of unused power. But protected by the dominant myth and haunted by the specter of anarchy, contemporary political scientists are not disposed to look for alternatives beneath accredited structures. Failure to acquiesce in the surface reality—the textbooks imply—is to invite disaster.

If academic political science has formulated no theory promising political renewal, neither have other critics of the dominant culture. In Paris in May 1968, Charles Newman let himself be swept along with French students to occupy l'Odéon. The youthful audience swarmed onto the stage while someone screamed, "Every man's an actor; every man's an artist." Newman was suddenly disconcerted: he felt he was witnessing what he later called "the absolute impossibility of our own renewal":

That utterly random free flow from the seats to the stage, that reversal of the elements, is to no purpose save reversal itself. What has happened is precisely the opposite of its avowed aesthetic intention—rather than create a new dynamism, new relationships, the scene has been frozen hard, indelibly so; even the volunteerr performers with their pronounced lack of officiousness, their gentleness, do not make up for it. They are only the reverse negative of their enemies.[2]

It has become clear that the figures who presented themselves as countercultural in the 1960s wholly failed to provide a theoretical framework to distinguish them from the dominant culture. Reacting against manipulative and technological forces, they took no time to articulate a program beyond what was already established. Their acts expressed no new context to clarify

---

"Like there's this cat who lives in back of me and our heads just aren't together at all."

"What do you mean?"

"Like we can't relate our heads. He comes over and lays down these heavy raps."

"Like what?"

"I don't know. Like he just comes in all the time with this really heavy stuff and I don't understand his experience and he doesn't understand mine. Like he comes over when he's tripping, you know. And he puts down this very heavy number and his mind is so fucked up and I just get very uptight. The vibrations are really heavy, you know, and negative. We're just not together at all."

—A twenty-four-year-old female college graduate

---

their intentions. Where the dominant culture simply perpetuated anachronistic disciplines, the counterculture identified with Woodstock Nation, a festival that promised formless joy, an amorphous letting go, a falling free. It seemed sufficient, as Timothy Leary intoned, to drop out, tune in, and thereby turn on. But into what, precisely, one might be tuned before reaching some new high remained unsaid. The titles alone of Abbie Hoffman's *Revolution for the Hell of It* and Jerry Rubin's *Do It!* would seem to have spelled out their authors' political programs in full.

In its antitechnological mood, the counterculture was no less simplistic: opt for the moment and find happiness in survival. Go for basic food, organic homesteading, natural childbirth, free schools and free clinics, handicraft co-ops, and labor gift exchanges. The new technology, as advertised and exploited in *The Whole Earth Catalogue*, was to be one of simple, honest tools. The rewards of work would be immediate and self-evident; neither organizations nor machines need to mediate between need and gratification. This expectation, expressed in its most heady form by Theodore Roszak's *Where the Wasteland Ends* (1973), helped define the 1960s as a flight from politics, an effort to avoid stress and be "left alone." The new prophets, seers, metaphysicians, and theologians exalted tribalism and ethnicity. They celebrated feeling, intimacy, and spontaneity—all of it summed up by the emblem of Love. Goodman's *Growing up Absurd* (1960), Leary's *Politics of Ecstasy* (1965), Brown's *Love's Body* (1966), Laing's *Politics of Experience* (1967), Castaneda's *Teachings of Don Juan* (1968), Reich's *Greening of America* (1971)—these were appreciated for the way they displayed an innocence of power relations and a hostility toward politics. None provided a context for their author's appealing rage and energy. They were simply confident that once the concept of normalcy is abandoned, as R. D. Laing urged, one might move through convulsion and be born anew. The message seemed clear: individuals have been cheated by civilization and law. Needless walls and boundaries keep violating human nature. By nature, Norman O. Brown noted, man is One; by a kind of self-betrayal, man became divided. Confusing the parts with the whole, man became, in Marcuse's term, one-dimensional. Nevertheless, a nonpolitical formlessness—a new conscious-ness, as Charles Reich was to put it—could be counted on to emerge. The members of a new society of equals would be open to one another—mellow and nice, to use two of the catchwords of the day.

In a remarkable article, Peter Marin caught both the delight and the pain that could be anticipated when the self was surrendered so that Real Life could possess what might be left over:

It was all fine [Marin wrote] until we came to the end of class. Now, said the teacher, let us read back to one another what we have written. So they stood in their various places and tried to make sense of what they had done. No couplets. No moon and spoon. Instead, a batch of unreadable scrawls that were socially useless—for they could not be read aloud. Some began to cry, and others turned to me with betrayed or angry faces, for they had broken free and now there was no way to express what they had done within the rituals of their given world.

That is, in miniature, the experience of the young in America. Whatever is for them intense, liberating or real, puts them at odds with what surrounds them. Their own transformative experiences with one another and with drugs and sex draw them more deeply into an inner space where none of our popular wisdom makes usable sense. There is a loss there, of course; the terrible absolute loss of location in culture. When cultures are thriving and coherent, private experience and public wisdom coincide; one can go inward and discover in ecstasy and experience the shared sources of power and knowledge; cultural myths bind together and create a web of felt meaning.

It is almost as if the dissolution of our binding myths had thrown us into the unmanageable turbulence out of which myths formed. . . . That is where we have been thrown by the slant of the times; in and down to confront in ourselves the sempervirid archetypes and demons and energies from which with luck, we will make a new way of seeing and speaking.

All of it seems beyond our control.[3]

And it all seems beyond control simply because it is detached from symbols able to give direction to confusing, maddening experiences. Individuals are released to drift. Rejecting the prevailing order of things but not wanting to articulate alternatives that will allow their negativism to remain a going concern, they can do nothing but exalt an unstructured continuum of Nature

---

The real Thanksgiving feast is offered on the first band [*of the Rolling Stone's* Let It Bleed], *titled "Gimme Shelter." An obsessively lovely specimen of tribal rock, this richly textured chant is rainmaking music. It dissolves the hardness of the Stones and transforms them into spirit voices singing high above the maxey figures of the dancing ground. The music takes no course, assumes no shape, reaches no climax; it simply repeats over an endless drone until it has soaked its way through your soul.*

—Albert Goldman

---

and Earth. Their utopia is but a formless Other in which all who had been made sick, lonely, and desperate by liberalism can finally get lost.

That the reaction to liberalism should be offered as an unformed ache for innocence is understandable enough: the dominant culture accommodates and exploits opposition so efficiently that no structure independent from it can emerge and affirm itself. Washed-out blue jeans, literature in disassembled bits and pieces, or muckraking books-of-the-month are simply absorbed in the market place of liberalism. And what remains outside the market is too thin—too private and nonpolitical—to be publicly effective.

The difficulty of *formulating* a countercultural position has been especially evident in contemporary art. Protests against prevailing ways of viewing the world are either assimilated by becoming merchandisable products or else so idiosyncratic that they have no durable impact. Even so energetic a movement as action painting turned out to be little more than an endless series of groundless acts of self-affirmation. Presenting themselves as pugnacious and willful performers, painters such as Jackson Pollock, Frank Kline, and David Smith used their large-scale works as weapons and lived their role as fighters, womanizers, and drinkers. None articulated a communal basis that might have constituted the ground for their self-expression. The self-indulgence displayed by the arts was revealed in Richard Poirier's *The Performing Self* (1971), an astute essay which came to focus on Norman Mailer. Sympathetic to Mailer, it still made clear that his turning from novelist to political candidate to public demonstrator to journalist was but an endless posturing because it communicated no shareable ground for his advertisements for himself. For Mailer and countless performers with less virtuosity, protest remained subjective, its underlying order invisible.

And yet the subjectivism characteristic of the reactions against the narrowness of liberal institutions reveals more than the presence of energy for renewal. Less clearly, it shows an inarticulate longing for a rebirth, for a new *form* of politics, for whatever structure might sustain *continuous* acts of self-expression. It is this still implicit concern, I think, that can be made explicit and serve for building a public order beyond liberalism.

To bring this order to light is not without risks, for it constitutes an affirmation of disaffection and annihilation. Yet were it to be recognized in all its dimensions it would make politics not only more difficult but also more rewarding. Until Americans risk giving explicit recognition to structures of language and politics which test more of themselves, they will feel the contemporary crisis but cannot grasp its meaning. Forever enrolled in introductory courses, forever memorizing the well-established "facts of political life," they will be sensitive to rules rather than to exceptions, to decisions made rather than to losses suffered. Lacking metaphors as well as communities for relating new realities, they cannot succeed in doing more than vaguely to apprehend the life they fail to live, the politics they might yet experience.

America may have lost its innocence, but so far nothing expressed and constructed at its center can give rise to a new life and a new politics. Nothing teases out some living form beneath the explosions and implosions of the present. For all their concerns with themselves, Americans do not allow themselves to relate familiar experiences to the still ungoverned spaces in which they are lost and in agony. They are apprehensive walkers in the city of today, but do not know how to formulate what they feel. As they write their accounts or speak their minds, they keep covering their tracks and erasing their errors. They emerge tearless, unstained, easily in control. They move in well-shaped circles, embracing a mythology that enables them to be chaste and undistracted even as their routines have worn thin. They are disconnected from experience which they vaguely feel is theirs—but is not quite theirs because no symbols have caught it, no words have related it.

Part Two

The Promise of
the Artist as Actor

"I'm still looking," she said. "Someone sure of himself."

"Jim was like that. He used to have lots of drive. Hot for certainties. Knew where he was headed and knew what was right. Worked on himself and straightened out the company. Kept working on me too. Always judging and doing things. Lots of excitement, but hard to take. Of course, he still knows what's right, but he's no longer sure. All the energy and toughness have gone out of him. Easier to live with though."

"But I'm looking for someone who's not judgmental at all."

"Sure—someone loose, easy, casual, nonchalant. Lets things go, drifts. But he'd still have one thing in common with Jim: no energy."

"Well, yes, but he'd be comfortable. Easy to live with."

4

Redeeming the Reaction to Liberalism

Puzzled by the gap between ideal and performance and yet not quite accepting the gap as fated, Americans yearn for alternatives. While the custodians of the liberal order feel the threat of anarchy and strive to maintain the system, the citizenry is inaudibly disquieted. An array of small gestures, often merely a display of sullenness, testifies to the existence of a malaise. Not wholly absorbed in their routines, Americans seek outlets for their discontents. In the process, they tend to react by abandoning the realm of politics altogether and decline to communicate. Yet, however muted and incoherent, their various reactions are not mere irrational reflexes. They may also be seen as deflected efforts to say *something*. Feeling they have no stake in their country, their job, or their neighborhood, the disaffected are still somehow impelled to give some shape and meaning to their malaise by making it known to others. But even while the Liberal Myth promises them room for self-expression, this room is so private that it invites boredom and silence.

Although the public sector is thereby devitalized, this is not regarded by liberals as a basic flaw of the system. The consequent absence of policy innovation, the failure of institutions to be responsive to social changes, and the reduction of politics to administration are seen as departures from an authentic liberalism. A dynamic, experimental posture, it is conceded, may well be repressed in the public sector. Inequities of power may well be perpetuated. The difference between Democrats and Republicans may well be superficial. Public ground for identifying and relating new interests may have eroded. But all this is seen as a welter of disconnected aberrations. Beneath appearances, an untarnished ideal is said to remain.

Yet it is this ideal itself that can be seen to thwart the emergence of more

> *Contemporary liberalism does not depreciate emotion in the abstract,*
> *and in the abstract it sets great store by variousness and possibility. Yet,*
> *as is true of any other human entity, the conscious and the unconscious*
> *life of liberalism are not always in accord. So far as liberalism is active*
> *and positive, so far, that is, as it moves toward organization, it tends to*
> *select the emotions and qualities that are most susceptible of organiza-*
> *tion. As it carries out its active and positive ends it unconsciously limits*
> *its view of the world to what it can deal with, and it unconsciously tends*
> *to develop theories and principles, particularly in relation to the nature*
> *of the human mind, that justify its limitation.*
>
> —Lionel Trilling

various interests. The notion prevails that thanks to a line drawn long ago, political and nonpolitical life are rightly separated. Furthermore, the failure to respect this separation by allowing private matters to become public would simply liberate the least scrupulous elements of the population. Naked human will, as James Madison proclaimed, would triumph. Surely a devitalized politics is preferable to the brutal wars of man in the state of nature. Once the hard-won ground for discriminating between politics and nature is given up, civilization itself will be destroyed. It therefore becomes imperative to hold the line separating political from nonpolitical life. What is more, any new effort to redefine this line must be recognized not as a political act but instead as a prepolitical revolutionary effort of *founding*—of creating some new public order. Such an effort is clearly needless: all the "essential" creative work was completed in the eighteenth century when it was duly settled what constitutes the arena of political life. Interests excluded at that time properly remain excluded today. They are private, not part of the shared order of man's common existence.

It follows that new private ventures must either remain private or can be permitted to emerge only after being cut down to predefined dimensions. They must be "reasonable." Dissidents who nevertheless seek to make their private interests public "engage in violence" or "stage a riot." Their appearance constitutes a "scene" that needs to be managed. Aren't all *legitimate* interests already public?

No doubt conflicts of interest are in fact negotiated within the channels of liberal politics. But the only interests deemed worthy of negotiating are established task-oriented ones. Only technique-centered, instrumentalist, utilitarian activities are seen to fit an *a priori* form of respectability. Thus liberalism provides opportunities for promoting one's interests—but only for people who have "clearly" defined goals and work "rationally" to achieve them. There is no well-lit room for actions whose sole justification is their presence in their own peculiar form. Neither the liberal imagination nor liberal politics accommodates men and women who wish *merely* to appear, who move into courts and legislative chambers and administrative hearing rooms *merely* to be in action.

When liberalism lives up to its ideal, the various institutions organized under its banner tend to dissolve new interests rather than to integrate them within an enlarged balance. Not only the party system but also the mass media, medical and psychoanalytic practice, and even grammar as taught in the schools are organized so as to reduce the range of expressed concerns. Individuals are left diminished—at once less destructive and less creative. They are systematically adjusted to life styles they loathe by procedures which cause them to feel embarrassed by their feeling of loathing. As a result, interests excluded from the established balance tend to atrophy from disuse. Kept off the record, relegated to cloakrooms, touched on only backstairs, they remain out of sight and unrelated. If, then, liberalism does succeed in relating and containing Americans, it does not relate and contain very much of them. It fulfills its design by directing the individual to repress, to aim for some prefigured true purpose, to do manifest good and avoid manifest evil, to pull himself together and keep his eye on the ball. Think ahead, the individual keeps telling himself. Stop playing around. Amount to something. An underlying taboo on playing pointless games, on being merely creative or merely reflective, gives a bad name to public activities designed merely to keep going. Not finishing—a preoccupation with mere process—is disparaged. If a public-spirited citizen such as Benjamin Franklin is appreciated, it is for his achievements, not for his constant quitting one job and moving on to another. While liberalism reserves space for play and politics, those who spend their lives in such spaces come to feel guilty. Knowing it is *better* to earn money or capture positions, they unconsciously convert play and politics into profit-making schemes. Not satisfied with merely keeping the game going, they come to confine playful activities to night hours and back alleys. If they have energy and curiosity left over after "serious" work, they move underground. Thus the disappointments and frustrations of liberalism give rise to the dirty story, the cult of bohemianism, the gratuitous act of defiance, the infuriated rebel lashing out against others and himself.

A compulsive instrumentalism which makes people into economic beings forever driven to calculate their advantages will remain the stock in trade of liberal regimes so long as we fail to raise our sights to discern a greater human potential. Raising our sights means looking within ourselves for more possibilities than the Myth of Liberalism allows: it means acting as if we had a potential for relating a greater diversity of interests. The ground for such action is the assumption that *everyone strives to be recognized in action*. All individuals adopt strategies for displaying themselves as attractive to others. Even near defeat, they will still clamor to be heard and seen. Assuming the value of this disposition, we rightly encourage active rather than reactive qualities within ourselves and others. Concerned with redeeming what liberalism represses, we properly let our own acts of seeing and of expressing what we see give credibility to the capacities for action which remain incipient, on the verge of being realized. We should take every opportunity to free deflected interests within ourselves and others and thereby realize ourselves in action. Realizing is thus simultaneously to comprehend and to make real; seeing a new order of reality is creating it.

Wanting to give recognition to the extremes of hardness and softness which lie unloved at the edge of our consciousness, we must seek to *accompany* those extremists in our midst who are compulsively driven toward some ultimate end. We must seek to give form to their unspoken desire to be deprived of their compulsiveness, to be slowed down, and to be acclaimed as members of the community. To treat individuals, including ourselves, as if their diverse outbursts and withdrawals are disguised declarations of citizenship is to establish the noneconomic, noncalculating dimension of America. It is to provide ground for an expressive politics. By appreciating the unacclaimed, repressed capacities of extremists, we are in effect recovering our lost communal dimensions. We bring the surface of our lives into relation with its subsurface undercurrents. We encourage old people to come in touch with their infantile impulses, adolescents to accept their craving for discipline, students to admit to their desire to teach, patients to diagnose themselves, reactionaries to recognize their own generous sensibilities.

Such political action which enlarges the balance of our interests is not only inherently rewarding. Today it has also become indispensable for human survival. Our very future is in question unless we draw on resources that go to waste in the liberal order. We can no longer afford to classify *anything* as

---

Nothing in existence may be subtracted, nothing is dispensable. . . .

—Friedrich Nietzsche

---

wild, dirty, perverse, or irrational in order to deny it the opportunity to play a part on what is becoming a global stage. Thus a psychologist, Robert E. Ornstein, has rightly noted how fundamentally the liberal ideology threatens survival—and what fundamental changes are necessary to meet the threat it poses:

> The analytic mode in which there is separation of objects, of the self from others (I-it relationship), has proved useful in individual biological survival, yet this mode apparently evolved to fit the conditions of life many thousands of years

ago. The evolution of culture proceeds much more quickly than biological evolution; so the analytic mode may not be as all-important a criterion for our contemporary Western society as it once was. The awareness of separation was a great advantage when survival threatened an individual's existence; for instance, one could isolate an enemy animal, kill it, and use it for food. However, this basic need, for individual survival, is no longer quite so basic for many in the West. After all, most of us now buy our food; we do not need to hunt for it . . . the survival problems now facing us are collective rather than individual: problems of how to prevent a large nuclear war, pollution of the earth, overpopulation. And notice that in these examples, a focus on individual consciousness, individual survival, works against, not for, a solution. A shift toward a consciousness of the interconnectedness of life, toward a relinquishing of the "every man for himself" attitude inherent in our ordinary construction of consciousness, might enable us to take those "selfless" steps that could begin to solve our collective problems. Certainly our culture has too severely emphasized the development of only one way of organizing reality. Perhaps at this point in time we can begin to see that the complementary mode can have survival value for our culture as a whole.[1]

Perhaps, says Ornstein, we can change our lives and begin to see. But given the exhaustion of available justifications for changing our lives, on what grounds? What model of success can orient us?

5

The Model of
Romanticism

The comforting belief that there are, after all, real beginnings and real endings, that some things are truly settled, serves to keep us from acknowledging our need to break boundaries and enlarge the range of our experience. Mind-forged manacles, as William Blake called them, keep us from questioning established reality. There are good reasons, one must concede, for respecting our constraints and being cautious before turning, as I am doing, to the theory and practice of Romanticism for help in breaking them. The polemics of Romanticism certainly do not inspire confidence. Enraged by oppression, Romantics from Rousseau to Nietzsche have continuously overstated the case for violating convention and freeing man's creative potential. As we read them and as we take note of the bloody enterprises of their followers, we become impressed by their impulse to annihilate, their nihilistic drive to escape the present. We come to be persuaded that in the world of Romanticism nothing but motion and emotion is certain. Romantics would seem to threaten not merely liberalism but the whole of our cultural enterprise. Their claim seems so total, in fact, that they would appear to legitimate no durable relationships whatever—certainly no politics to control the rage they release. Notoriously, they failed to reflect on the need for political institutions—*any* institutions. They drafted no constitution to make going concerns out of the revolutions they promoted. Alienated from conventional politics, they left an ominous gap.

We are rightly made nervous by the eagerness of Romantics to move into spontaneity and anarchy. Notoriously, they courted madness, cruelty, terror, and death. Moreover, we know that the very individuals who argue for convulsion keep losing their nerve and support the imposition of some ultimate synthesis. When the movements of Romanticism have not led to some terminal frenzy they have been aborted by dictatorial regimes. Yet while this is true and needs to be admitted, it is no less important to stress that the exponents of a new consciousness and a new politics were never committed to any particular settlement—only to keeping as much of life unsettled as one can bear. If like Nietzsche or Lawrence they recurrently became elitist, the cause was that they came to believe that the mass of men simply did not have the psychological and economic resources for bearing the freedom for which a host of Romantics clamored. Moreover, they failed to trouble themselves with giving an institutional basis to their overriding concern—the freeing of man's creative energies. Yet there is no reason why Romanticism should not be understood to include whatever practices assure a *continuous* breaking of boundaries and settlements. These practices, I think, should be regarded as distinctively political.

There can be no question that the projects underwritten by Romanticism generate disorder. They impose ever-new perspectives—that is, ever-new places where lines are expected to meet. They deny the assumption that some fixed, discernible purpose inheres in our lives and that, when all is well, we will organize and govern ourselves to conform to it. For the Romantic, process replaces te: ·ology: it is best never to get anywhere at all. In the end, nothing comes of anything.

This view of the inconsequence of our activities is not wholly unknown in the world of liberalism. After all, the very rich (who do not *have* to amount to anything) and the very poor (who have given up trying) incorporate it in their lives. And the preponderant majority which lives in between knows of all sorts of inconsequential affairs in places which liberalism marks off as

---

When we say that we aspire to only one end, namely to eliminate all ends, we are saying something paradoxical. Yet the paradox is readily resolved. Something quite general is meant when we say "we aspire to only one end"; and we mean quite specific ends when we refer to ends we want to eliminate. Unfortunately, whether we speak of the general or the specific, we use the same term. While we may be confusing when we say that our general objective is never to embrace any specific one, we ourselves are not confused.

—Robert Claridge

---

private, places in which it is occasionally possible to discern projects based on a paradoxical concern: their purpose would seem to be to dispense with purpose. Whether these affairs are a game of tennis, an academic conference, a transaction between businessmen, a walk in the woods, or a theatrical performance, they do not aim at realizing some externally given end. They are pursued for their own sake; their goal resides in the action itself.

In its most concentrated form—the form I am here idealizing so as to clear the ground for a postliberal politics—this absence of extrinsic purpose is characteristic of artistic projects. The artist's ventures seem most clearly

---

"My fantasy of making the perfect movie is very, very simple. You have an idea for a film, you work with a screenwriter of a playwright—it can be either a film or a play—you get a marvelous inventive director, and you cast it the way it ought to be cast, not because you have to cast it a certain way. You get together and you have four incredible weeks of rehearsal and then you shut it down. And no one ever sees it. That would be a marvelous movie. You never crank a foot of film and you never have an audience to come in and see it."

—Paul Newman

---

opposed to the achievement of anything that might be confused with usable products, with anything the dominant culture refers to as "good." To be sure, the artist keeps appearing in the market place of the liberal society; he produces profitable merchandise, buildings that attract tenants, plays that sell. But underground, he remains a restless figure forever demonstrating how one's life can acquire meaning not in projects completed, awards won, certificates earned, or subjects finally mastered—not in finishing—but rather in the creative process itself. "My job," Robert Altman has said about his role of film director, "is not to create a work of art, but to reflect on the process of it."[1]

When we see the artist comprehensively we recognize how much implicated he is in what is a social activity. He is involved with others even when he is alone and converses with no one but his alter ego. He ineluctably finds himself moving within a community of fellow artists, curators, critics, collectors, patrons, connoisseurs, and spectators—his public. This involvement is the case as much for novelists or sculptors as it is for the members of a movie company, a surgical team, a private school, or a garden club. All of these may be perceived as in the process of performing for one another. True, a surgeon may seem more interested in some end result: a successful operation or a larger income, just as a novelist may aspire to write a "classic" or a best seller. Neither may seem satisfied merely to display his talents. Yet in the form revealed by those we recognize as artists, the displaying of one's self in action—or having one's finished work exhibit only the processes that led to it—is excuse enough for one's activities.

The artist—again, as I am idealizing him—will forever call the attention of others to as much of himself as he can bring into play. François Truffaut's "Day for Night" (1973) elaborately illustrates how *more than anything else* the immediate collaborative activity itself matters. In this film about the making of a film, everyone's effort focuses on the pleasurable, sunny, dexterous company itself, on its infinite promises, on the intricate relations among members of the crew, technicians, producers, and actors, on film-making in general—the very title referring to shooting night scenes in the daylight with filters. Playing the roles of actors and nonactors, all are dead serious about acting. Truffaut's movie is an homage to the artifice, to the medium itself, to the way soap bubbles become snow. In the end, there is but

---

All process oriented works rely on the viewer and the art critic for their final definition as works of art. If it is neither photographed nor written about, it disappears back into the environment and ceases to exist. Many serious artists, at this time, are for the most part involved in making art-producing systems. The works themselves are not to be considered as art.

—Les Levine

---

a tenuous effervescent presentation of resources for continuous living, of movement without transcendent purpose or ulterior motive.

In her review of Robert Altman's "Nashville" (1975), Pauline Kael conveys what is involved in such a venture:

He dissolves the frame, so that we feel the continuity between what's on the screen and life off-camera. . . . "Nashville" is, above all, a celebration of its own performers. . . . There's no single reason why anybody does anything in this movie. . . . There are no real denouements, but there are no loose ends, either: Altman doesn't need to wrap it all up, because the people here are too busy being alive to be locked in place. . . . Altman has what Joyce had: a love of the supreme juices of everyday life. He can put unhappy characters on the screen and you don't wish you didn't have to watch them; you accept their unhappiness as a piece of the day, as you do in "Ulysses." You don't recoil because Altman wants you to be part of the life he shows you and to feel the exhilaration of being alive. When you get caught up in his way of seeing, you no longer anticipate what's coming. . . .[2]

None of this looseness to avoid becoming captivated by dominant values —indeed *any* values—is a mere letting go and falling free. The artist may write at degree zero, paint white on white, compose resounding silences, use nonrepressive prose to celebrate the nonrepressive society, blueprint empty analytical frameworks, or play games without rules. He may draw us toward the spaces beyond the door held open by R. D. Laing—toward the agraphia of Rimbaud or the desperate negations of Nietzsche. But to save that aspect of ourselves which allows us to feel the pleasures of being observed and esteemed in action, he also provides for beads to pray with and count on, fixtures by which to get one's bearing, frames and perspectives to direct our movement. Knowing we can salvage nothing without form, he conforms to a discipline which the exponents of Romanticism called for and which we might yet treat as model for a new politics. Crystallized in works of art and implicit in the aesthetics of Romanticism, such a model promises to give significance to experiences repressed by the politics of liberalism.

The artist's discipline places into doubt whatever he (and we along with him) have come to experience as real beyond doubt. Though not necessarily in sequence, he surveys reality, breaks it up, and reconstructs it. He disrupts routines and multiplies relationships; he complicates the presumed exigencies of life and logic. In other words, he confronts the present state of things (himself included) but does not accept it as it appears to be—as complete, as having ended. He agitates it by adding questions not likely to have been previously asked. How would people behave under changed conditions? How would they perform on different stages? If we added new material to a familiar setting—a windfall of cash, unrequited love, a death in the family—how would familiar characters respond? What potentialities would be realized? What unfamiliar behavior would come into play?

In such interrogations, the artist treats conventional reality as ambiguous and proceeds to contradict it. Violating what is so clearly the case, he exhibits unknown possibilities, hidden capacities for action. Whether poems or communities of living men, works of art are thus experiments: they put existing worlds into crucibles and transform them under controlled pressure. Students are placed into a curriculum. A character is put on trial, Thomas Mann's Castorp into an alpine sanitarium, Bernard Malamud's Levin into the English Department of Cascadia College, Norman Mailer's protagonist on the steps of the Pentagon. All are pressured—and released in the end, orphans anew.

A greater range of possibilities for change is revealed by actors who themselves design the setting which allows them to develop and display their capacities. Thus Charlie Chaplin created endless occasions for testing his limits and sharing the results with others. Walter Kerr's account, which in the end also exposes the pathos of a limitless freedom to exhange roles, points to the range of Chaplin's possibilities:

> If he wishes to rescue a woman from a burning building his skill and bravery are unexampled; if he wishes to gamble he is at once a shark; if he is inducted as soldier, he can capture the Kaiser. He can farm, play a violin, cope with bullies, duel as Fairbanks duelled. He can be a woman seductively. . . . Ask him to be a

homosexual, he will be homosexual. . . . The secret of Chaplin as a character is that he can be anyone. The dark pain filling Chaplin's eyes . . . comes from the hopeless limitation of having no limitations.[3]

At its most persuasive and powerful, the possibilities for remaining in action and displaying the impact of action on the actor are exemplified in the lives of performers who seem to have no private roles whatever. Thus Malraux, Duchamp, Godard, Muhammad Ali, Mailer, and Mishima have blatantly included themselves in their field of action, communicating not only what they do but also what transpires in their minds. They have shown themselves opening up, taking things in, and changing in the process of observing. In each instance, as they have exhibited themselves to us, they have become the spokesmen of the smothered elements in our lives as well. They have represented suppressed realms of being. They have made familiar scenes (and our knowledge of them) vibrate so intensely that these scenes have become disjointed—thereby free us to rejoin them differently. Their transactions have shown that we, too, can break the dense inevitability of the way we happen to be. Committed to the proposition that the truth lies only in the ineffable, incommunicable whole, they imply that *our* truths are only so-called truths, mere surfaces and fragments.

Artistic performances generate tensions which we can resolve only by becoming alive to new ways of viewing the world. They detach us from old ways. They change our loyalties. De-eroticizing our old involvements, they alienate us from whatever objectives we have embraced with singular intensity—whether it is money, sex, status, pleasure, or power. Thus the artist jeopardizes the powers that be, the obstacles to self-expression, the forces which block sympathy and love. He identifies excesses—excesses of domination and submission, of sensory input and sensory deprivation. In the name of unnamed and therefore unknown experience, he seeks to loosen the hold of named and known experience. His campaigns are designed to be disruptive; they are organized to remove blockages in life, perception, and utterance. Accordingly, solidified identities are disintegrated by the interminable flow of words of Mailer or Joyce, by the sparse, helpless gestures of Beckett, or by the deflections of Pinter, by authors who end for the sole reason that they are helpless to do otherwise.

The moment the artist is captivated by any end whatever, the aesthetics of Romanticism demand that he detach himself from it, that he treat it as puerile, fatuous, and flat, as threat to his being. He is induced to abandon his conventional sense of beauty or fitness by being made to realize that no creative act, finally, is really good enough. Thus Henry Adams writes again and again that he can write nothing, or Rimbaud ceases at the age of twenty-one to write poetry altogether, or Beckett uses all his ingenuity so as to appear finished, dry, and mute. Wittgenstein, like Nietzsche, elaborately travels toward the void—willing it—and Marx, while straining to arrive at a political destination, takes care not to identify it. "We need transmitters of information,"

> *The creation of paintings and sculptures is considered by artists to be*
> *a confinement of the creative impulse. "There are already enough*
> *objects," says a conceptualist,"and there is no need to add to those that*
> *exist."*

> —Harold Rosenberg

Hans Erich Nossack has one of his characters write, "who know how to keep their mouths shut."

Yet even as he affirms nothing, merely tilting the world and altering current perspectives, the artist cannot help but reveal the stable ground on which he acts. Beneath the shifting surface of his projects, he allows for indications of how he brings the extremes of our existence into relation. He allows us to see by what *measures* we enlarge the context for each of those familiar self-contained polarities of experience which in their isolation—their sheer idiocy—become our dead ends:

Order	Chaos
Form	Substance
Reason	Emotion
Professionalism	Amateurism
Individualism	Fraternalism
Urban	Rural
Calculation	Spontaneity
Constraint	Freedom
Thanatos	Eros
Tightness	Looseness
Sequential	Simultaneous
Day	Night
Elimination	Absorption
Destruction	Creation
Detachment	Attachment
Classic	Romantic
Head	Heart
Mind	Body
Male	Female
End	Beginning

Whenever these absolutes are about to claim our *full* attention, the artist redistributes our feelings about them, detaching us, for example, from genital sex or established power centers and attaching us to unappreciated zones of our existence. He threatens privileged orders. As Hayden White has noted, every avant garde opposes entrenched elites—

> whether of privileged positions in space (as in the old perspectival painting and sculpture), of privileged moments in time (as one finds in the older narrative art of fiction and in conventional historiography), of privileged places in society, of privileged areas in the consciousness (as in the conservative, that is to say, orthodox Freudian psychoanalytic theory), of privileged parts of the body (as the genitally organized sexual lore insists is "natural"), or of privileged positions in culture (on the basis of a presumed superior "taste") or in politics (on the basis of a presumed superior "wisdom").[4]

The artist redeploys interests by creating new arenas within which our focus is changed. How deliberately Godard's films seek to do this by involving his audiences is shown by Alfred Willener's interpretation:

> A cinema in which fiction and documentary are mixed, in which the intentions of the author/director go well beyond anything that could be expressed in his usually very summary plots—Godard's films, his more recent ones at least, are not enclosed within the beginning and end recounted by the author, but are rather 'slices' cut from the lives of the characters represented—a cinema of this kind is not well suited to traditional discursive continuity. Indeed, Godard rejects such continuity from the outset—rejects the hypnotic *fascination* of the film that plunges the spectator into a world from which he re-emerges only when the words 'The End' appears on the screen. Neither *La Chinoise* nor *2 ou 3 choses que je sais d'elle* contains a single sequence that allows more than a few seconds' passive reception. The incoherence with which Godard has been reproached, even if it may sometimes seem excessive even to his admirers, is often the result of a desire to prevent the audience from being lulled into torpor, to force it to participate in some way, if only by means of irritation. Just as Godard, he tells us, watches himself making his films as he is shooting them, the spectator is forced to watch himself seeing the film. Because he participates in the actual shooting, he must, in a sense, follow the same itinerary as the director. In *La Chinoise* particularly—a cartoon presented at the beginning of the first reel, warns us that it is 'a film still in the making'—all continuity is dispensed with: the clapperboy and camera crew appear on the screen, the actors are sometimes 'in the film' and sometimes outside it, sometimes they speak directly to the spectator (which may give one the impression that one is the director with whom the actor is speaking), sometimes they answer questions put to them by an interviewer who appears on the set. The film operates constantly on several levels. Indeed, it is quite striking to see, in discussions afterwards, how very different certain sequences appeared to different spectators, each one placing particular emphasis on one of the levels offered by the director. In this sense, Godard's films are not, as is often said, slapdash from a technical point of view, but on the contrary highly planned. In Godard's films, none of those 'alien', unintentional sights and sounds, which are usually excluded from studio shooting, and whose exclusion is responsible for the hypnotic fascination mentioned earlier, are eliminated. It may be irritating when part of a dialogue is

drowned by the noise of a motor-cycle or a pneumatic drill, but Godard does not claim to have made a finished work, but rather a *sketch* of a piece of a reality that one does not have to be a film director to see. The Godard method is based on a desire to 'demythify' the art and technique of the cinema. As François Truffaut puts it, Godard has 'fichu la pagaille' in the cinema and made it possible for France 'to become a country of forty-five million film directors'. Not, of course, that all technical limitations are eliminated. Godard has simply introduced, into a field where they did not previously exist, as much for financial as for artistic reasons, improvisation and the 'unfinished'.

As Godard has frequently explained, his method does not involve total improvisation at the time of shooting; it necessitates a great deal of preparation and a thorough soaking in the subject. 'I make my film', he says 'when I'm dreaming, having lunch, reading, talking to you now.' This preparation is not intended to preclude the unexpected, but, on the contrary, to allow greater freedom during the actual shooting. And neither this shooting nor the film presented to the public is regarded as the culmination of a creative process, but rather as a stage in that process. In this respect, Godard represents the antithesis of a certain aesthetic of the French cinema whose prototype might be said to be the work of René Clair, who is reported to have said: 'My film is almost finished—all I have to do now is to shoot it.' It would be interesting—but difficult—to know how much each participant contributed, not to the making, but to the actual shaping of the film. Without going so far as to speak of collective work, it could be said that *2 ou 3 choses que je sais d'elle*, for example, is a case in which a large degree of autonomy was left to the actor (for this film, the principal actress had no script to learn in advance and sometimes had to reply, during the shooting, to unexpected questions put to her by the director through a miniature ear-phone).

In an article on *Une femme mariée*, made in 1964, J. Doniol-Valcroze wrote that it would be possible to assemble all Godard's films to form a *film-fleuve* lasting several hours, in which each character could intervene in a story to which he did not belong, and wander in and out of the re-edited whole without any sense of incongruity. The spectator of a Godard film is in a similar situation. He wanders in and out of the film rather than observes it. He can see one sequence from the inside, another from the outside, without losing anything of the essential experience, dwell on a particular scene, then 'skip' others. The editing, which is never discursive, and in which speed alternates with slowness, 'interesting' moments with 'boring' ones (which need not be the same for every spectator), helps him to do this by presenting him with choices: to select, to see, to listen, or to see and to listen. This produces what might be called an aleatory participation that often goes beyond the intentions of the creator. Each sequence becomes an object, as J. Doniol-Valcroze remarks, independent of the rest of the film, which may be looked at 'from many different points of view' and experienced 'in an autonomous duration'. The meaning of these objects is not imposed at the outset; it is built up by projection onto a body of information supplied by the director.

It is obviously not my intention to make Godard the precursor of new forms of culture that were to emerge in May. And one can readily accept certain criticisms that have been made of his work. It cannot be denied that it is often ambiguous. Some (including himself?) see him as a Maoist, others as a left-wing or right-wing anarchist, or perhaps even as an 'ambidextrous' anarchist—in any case, he cannot easily be labelled. Is he naïve and pretentious, a genius and mediocre, sincere and cunning? Godard may be all these at once. Nevertheless, his films represent a break with the conformism of an art that is as rich in possibilities as it is unimaginative and, according to some, subjected to an aesthetic terrorism. Godard's main contribution is perhaps in having inverted the terms of a rule that subjected the mind to the form by tending to put the form entirely at the service of the idea to be conveyed, without regard to the 'beautiful' and the 'logical'. Even if, for reasons that cannot be attributed entirely to him, he has only partly succeeded, his work has challenged the notion of cinema spectacle, and therefore a certain image of culture, the relations between the creator and his public.[5]

Richard Schechner, founder of New York City's Performance Group, has similarly changed the relation between creator and public so as to activate passive spectators. He converted "found space"—streets, warehouses, mountainsides, meadows—into theatrical space, using it to heighten the experience of both actors and spectators, enabling them through deliberately designed rituals to reach a higher state of self-awareness. He made each performance a *rite de passage* through which all participants were to be transformed. On entering the theater to see "Dionysus in 69," each spectator is separated from whomever he accompanies so that he must make a separate entry. For "Commune," the audience must surrender its shoes when entering. For "Makbeth," the audience moves through a maze before climbing down into the playing area. *Everyone* involved is a protagonist. Everyone

---

Norman Mailer's commitment to dialectics means that he includes materials which threaten the symmetry of any possible form. His is the art of not arriving. . . . In him there is on one hand the marvelously fastidious stylist, a writer almost precious in his care for phrasing and cadence, and on the other hand seemingly at odds, the boisterous, the vulgar actor. . . . Solidification is not the function of Mailer's art and is instead ascribed to those forces in contemporary civilization to which his art opposes itself. With what seems to be at times obtuseness, he chooses to put his stress of appreciation on those aspects of a subject which anyone working in the rationalist, humanist, liberal tradition would generally choose to ignore or condemn.

He makes the point that an artist who does not bring in art those qualities which might disrupt formal coherence is guilty of doing to art, and to culture, what Eisenhower did to politics during what were for Mailer the worst years of his time in America: "He did not divide the nation as a hero might (with a dramatic dialogue as a result); he merely excluded one part of the nation from the other."

—Richard Poirier

---

must choose how extensively to participate, go through some agony, and see his stable conventions tested by alternatives. The artist as theater director provides space for encounters. He wounds sensibilities, slaps at coherence, creates an open space where none had been suspected. He instructs everyone —including himself—to court misfortune, to let go of familiar pains and pleasures so that it becomes possible to master more of both. He adds modifiers to beliefs we had come to regard as settled. His distinctive discipline consists of systematically undercutting what he appears to assert, scrupulously displacing and reversing himself, destroying well-known plots and sequences, implying the opposite of what he affirms. "The artist," Erich Heller has noted, "woos even with his aggressions, seduces even with his chastity, seeks the admiration of those he dooms in his apocalyptic visions, and the applause of those he damns with his last judgments."[6] He leads himself and others to see the teacher as student, the doctor as patient, the hero as villain, the fool as sage. The techniques he employs show wardens to be their own prisoners and the rich to lead impoverished lives. They show good causes—like evil ones—to have another side. They make it inconceivable for life to be merely what it is: they make it just as inconceivable for life to be merely otherwise. Whether assertive or seductive, the artist's work gives indubitable villains and heroes their moments of doubt.

The artist enables us to realize that no parts of reality are settled—not even by him. Leaving traces of his own presence, letting on that his vision is *distinctively* his, he implies it is *merely* his and that others might proceed differently and establish different realities. Leaving the frame vague and the center ambiguous, he insinuates that not even *his* expressions settle the boundary and meaning of a situation, that society might draw new boundaries and create new meanings. Harold Rosenberg has reported on the consequences of this posture:

> Painting, sculpture, drama, music have been undergoing a process of de-definition. The nature of art has become uncertain. At least, it is ambiguous. No one can say with assurance what a work of art is—or, more important, what is not a work of art. . . . The artist without art, the beyond-art artist, is not an artist at all, no matter how talented he may be as an impressario of popular spectaculars. The de-definition of art necessarily results in the dissolution of the figure of the artist, except as a fiction of popular nostalgia. In the end everyone becomes an artist.[7]

The thrust toward equality is manifest in every particular element of the artist's operation. By including flaws and irritants, he detaches spectators from his work, and activates them to encompass and appropriate more of reality, to enlarge their own cramped lives. He enables them to become creators of new realities. He first attracts them by indicating (in documentary fashion) that something really is "out there" and then alienates them by refusing to place things out there so definitively that they might believe him and let him have the last word. He is trustworthy only insofar as his truth is not offered as such, insofar as it is advanced in the form of disclaimers and proclaims itself to be other than what it seems. He knows—to say it sententiously—what he does not know, and that others can trust him because he so clearly trusts no specific aspect of himself. Having concluded, he hastens to treat his conclusion lightly. He removes the heavy mysteries and taboos of the day by not caring too deeply, by not pursuing truth too intensely, by pretending to let truth come—and dismissing it in his very effort to share it. Thus jazz musicians will not let a composition become an entity separate from the performance. Their performing, as Alfred Willener has noted, is their only product. John Coltrane would call attention to his appearance, but not to

> A New York artist, Vito Acconci, periodically notifies the art world, by mail, that on certain dates he will mount a stool in his study x number of times and that this "work" may be viewed at the designated hours. . . . I report on Acconci without having seen him do his act. Why should anyone see him? That his art is exactly like anything else is the point of it.
>
> —Harold Rosenberg

anything else that might follow: he would leave the stage abruptly, acknowledging no applause. Allowing his composition to disintegrate, he affirmed nothing but himself in action. Rejecting pre-established musical structures, he made his own sounds, touched his own nature, and thereby revealed the ground he shared with others.[8] Similarly, Peter Townshend thought his "breaking-up routine" was his "biggest thing":

> When I was in art school I got wind of an auto-destructive artist named Gustav Metzger. That really blew my mind. So I introduced the idea of breaking up instruments as part of the finale of the show: with puffs of smoke and flashes of light. . . . Lots of people said: "That's terrible" and stuff like that. Some geezers thought we were cheapening our music. But it's not just the destruction of the instrument itself; it's the destruction of what you're actually doing. You actually destroy *everything*—you destroy the guitar, the group's musical line, you destroy the audience's mental participation.

In the end, when all goes well, we are confronted by absolutely nothing but our purged innocent selves.

This encounter with nothing—nothing but our own unused resources for creativity—becomes possible when the artist succeeds in making light of whatever stands in the way of his own dismissal. Like the ideal teacher or psychoanalyst, he expects to become expendable. Thus whatever he appears to be, he will seek to abandon, leaving the impression that he is forever taking the other side. Merely *appearing* as composed and truthful, he is but a prevaricator, *Doppelgänger*, or impersonator. He lets his very conduct deny the reality which meets the eye.

Yet even as he demystifies, the artist embraces not some amorphous vacuity but rather a state in which quite specific things are *known* to be absent because they had been previously experienced and overcome, a state in which healed wounds testify to the absence of heroic deeds and final solutions, impregnable armor and total victories. Because there can be no unmistakable clues to something which is *not* anything, it is easy to misread those who promise—and deliver—nothing. Disarming and desublimating, they would appear to offer merely emptiness, a formless existence. They seem to ask us to keep performing without discipline, protocol, and grammar. They may actually assail the very basis for their productivity and recognition—their museums, galleries, and markets—by producing nonproducts, digging grave-size ditches in Central Park (as Oldenburg has done), making sculptures of steam (Morris), submitting descriptions of nonexisting work (Heubler), painting with the beam of a flashlight (Picasso), hanging a curtain across a

---

STATEMENT OF ESTHETIC WITHDRAWAL

> The undersigned, Robert Morris, being the maker of the metal construction entitled Litanies, described in the annexed Exhibit A, hereby withdraws from said construction all esthetic quality and content and declares that from the date hereof said construction has no such quality and content.

—Robert Morris

---

valley (Christo), creating a work that destroys itself (Tinguely), designing a curtain of air (Asher), or attaching a label to a bench at the Whitney Museum (anonymous). Conceptions replace objects; media become mixed; music is decomposed.

Of course such efforts fail the moment they are recognized once again as Art, as when in 1973 the Whitney Museum solemnly announced that Mike Heiser would appear and remove four stone paving blocks from its sculpture court. Aware of such exploitation, the artist has no choice but to intensify his nonproductivity. His works become ever more silent and less significant. They move altogether beyond being useful, marketable, or pleasing. Risking loss of control and betrayal of his discipline, he edges toward an incomprehensible desert, expressing the mere "shimmering of chaos," as Cézanne wrote. He tests Mallarmé's strategy and writes *poésie pure* until he becomes transparent and weightless, until his rebellion finally expires. The traces he leaves become fragile portraits of the moment he happened to have abandoned his work. In itself—untouched by interpretation—his work amounts to nothing; it contains no lesson, tells no tale, gives no instruction. It makes clear only that life has not been comprehended, that all beginnings and

> *The entire system of grids which analysed the sequence of represen-*
> *tations (a thin temporal series unfolding in men's minds), arresting its*
> *movement, fragmenting it, spreading it out and redistributing it in a*
> *permanent table, all these distinctions created by words and discourse,*
> *characters and classification, equivalences and exchange, have been so*
> *completely abolished that it is difficult today to rediscover how that*
> *structure was able to function. The last "bastion" to fall—and the one*
> *whose disappearance cut us off from Classical thought forever—was*
> *precisely the first of all those grids: discourse, which ensured the initial,*
> *spontaneous, unconsidered deployment of representation in a table.*
> *When discourse ceased to exist and to function within representation as*
> *the first means of ordering it, Classical thought ceased at the same time*
> *to be directly accessible to us. . . .*
>
> *(What is language? What is a sign? What is unspoken in the world, in*
> *our gestures, in the whole enigmatic heraldry of our behavior, our*
> *dreams, our sicknesses—does all that speak, and if so in what language*
> *and in obedience to what grammar? Is everything significant, and, if*
> *not, what is, and for whom, and in accordance with what rules? What*
> *relation is there between language and being, and is it really to being*
> *that language is always addressed—at least, language that speaks truly?*
> *What, then, is this language that says nothing, is never silent, and is*
> *called "literature"?)*
>
> —Michel Foucault

endings are mere fantasies—full of sound and fury, yes, but nevertheless of no significance. As the distance between art and life is deliberately shortened, as spectators move closer to experiences, as authorship becomes meaningless, as high culture collapses, as a mass of interpreters is activated, and as rules for action become increasingly ambiguous and unpredictable—in short, as the artist succeeds—no one can remain sure of anything but his own elaborate intransigence in the face of finalities, his will to signal not for help, only for recognition.

Insofar as our judgments are grounded in a Romantic aesthetic, we will discount everything but acts of signaling. We will understand that the patterns we impose on the landscape or the shapes we give military formations are not dictates of necessity but efforts to communicate. Thus we realize that even as men nearly lose consciousness, they will still resolve to watch themselves and report on what is happening. Even at their most intoxicated, they will soberly assume a position outside of their experience and seek to make a scene for others.

That inaudible inner voice of Romanticism which says "watch yourself" may finally be recognized as the voice of civility, as the quintessence of politics. It is a voice which expresses our interest not in formless experience as such but in comprehending, symbolizing, and conveying what we feel. We honor this interest when we call attention to ourselves in action, knowing that all our life, as John Donne wrote, is but a going out to the place of execution, and a signaling on the way.

What distinguishes those who are acclaimed as creative in the arts and sciences is simply the intensity and inclusiveness of their signaling. Theirs is a concentrated and sustained determination to give significance to the accidental and mysterious forces which threaten our composure. Accepting the chance appearance of phenomena, they seek to relate them. They seek to establish the coherence of Times Square or Las Vegas, the beauty in crumpled fenders, the point of empty lives, the poetry in found objects, the connection among events without antecedents or consequences. To remain composed in the face of their perceptions, they create compositions that make their experience (and ours as well) assume manageable form. We therefore welcome the connections made by the dreamspeech of Joyce, the interrogations of Beckett, or the archetypes of Jung. In search of connections, we rightly scrutinize the odd languages of American Indians, Zen monks, Delphic oracles, and astrological charts. In search of new forms of communication, we are receptive to communities in which imperceptible gestures or ambiguous mandalas give point to our feelings, in which flowers speak and tigers burn, in which people beat drums, count beads, and hum primal tunes, in which it becomes possible to create an alchemy of hopelessness.

Lacking such an alchemy, we succumb to a world of either/or antipodes, stereotyping or mythologizing phenomena as either completely white or completely black. We acquiesce in some currently accepted notion of what is truly Male or Female, Doctor or Patient, Flower or Weed. Believing that the middle ground on which Romanticism seeks to bring opposites into relationship is inauthentic and compromising—and deploring inauthenticity and compromise—we let established absolutes usurp the time and space in which relations can grow. Revealing ourselves as single-minded nonpolitical beings, we become captives of sovereign finalities.

I realize that such a nonpolitical existence becomes attractive when we have lost our breath and cannot compose ourselves. Bewildered and near panic, we welcome stabilizers. Under such conditions, only idealized absolutes inspire confidence. They seem to free us from alien oppressors or from our own mindlessness. Because miracles, mysteries, and authorities give us no security, inquisitors like Dostoevsky's would always seem to have a case. Yet to surrender our freedom of choice is to betray that very consciousness which enables us to determine whether surrender continues to be justified. Having paid for security, we keep paying: singular abstractions designed by men long dead continue to keep us in a state of dependency. We lose the capacity for challenging what has become a necessity and learn to trust *real* statesmen, priests, doctors, psychiatrists, architects, or teachers. Finally, we treat churches, hospitals, prisons, schools, retirement centers, or corporations not as man-made settings but as the necessary condition of human life.

To remain in control of ourselves, we must be able to acknowledge continuously that nothing less than self-government based on self-knowledge will ever do, that it is quite *natural* for us to assume responsibility for ourselves and act in relation to what we know to be in our interest. We must insist that, despite all pressures on us to conclude, we desire to see ourselves in continuous action. For us, this claim can be no mere "point of view" or useful ideology. It must be treated as a nonideological, universal human disposition. All of us, it should be clear, are disposed to take action when aware of the deadening, boring banalities of our lives. Even the most benign structure of power is finally seen as offensive for no other reason than its sheer existence. Imperviously present, it begs to be assailed, to be measured and scaled and mastered because, like some alpine peak, it is so indubitably there. It should not *be*—for the sole reason that, for us, nothing whatever should finally be. What annoys is precisely its imperturbability, its obtuse, dumb, inane, sense-dulling presence. To quicken our own sensibilities, we have no choice but to test its power of resistance, to act upon putative reality, to violate the belief of whoever claims to know the true boundary between the realm of necessity and that of freedom.

To engage in such reality-violating ventures is to experience the pleasure inherent in gaining freedom from the present, from what has been *made* present, from all that which the powerful claim to be necessary, inevitable, logical, rational, factual, real, timely, clean, normal, or successful. Such self-liberating action reveals necessity to have been choice and success to have been incomplete. By transforming truths into half truths, it demystifies established myths. Engaged in such action, we dissolve alleged beginnings and endings into processes. We induce doctors merely to *act* as doctors or teachers merely to *act* as teachers. We emerge as no less *and as no more* than actors eager to play our diverse parts, never confusing any one of our parts with the whole. We relate whatever conclusions we may have reached to a larger context, thereby depriving them of their conclusiveness. Thus ugly becomes beautiful, wasteful becomes efficient, madness becomes sanity. Of course, the moment we have reached such new conclusions, we remain obliged to question them as well. We will feel the need to keep exposing unknown aspects of our existence until, in the end, we see that nothing holds firm except our wholly natural disposition to create always new perspectives for experiencing ourselves and others in action.

Ideally, works of art demonstrate how we can stand our ground and carry on even when we lose our footing. Inherently inconclusive and designed to maintain suspense, they train us to withstand the continuous pressure to make up our minds and become partisans of but one side. Induced by the artist to participate in his project, we learn to endure situations in which nothing would seem to fit, in which everything would seem deranged and unfinished. His work wounds and heals—and makes us look for further battles. It lets us live with tensions which—unrelated, unintegrated—would drive us out of our minds.

When artistic activities are seen as experimental probes that complicate prevailing orders and disclose alternatives, it becomes clear how they, like all forms of play, enable us to escape forces that oppress and diminish us— whether they are the forces of so-called nature or so-called politics. The experiments of art reduce the violence, exploitation, and cruelty in our midst simply because they oppose conditions that dull our senses. They extend contexts by making specific situations less flat, monotonous, simple, banal, and familiar. They move us away from sensory deprivation and loneliness— all blocked eroticisms.

It is precisely within the open spaces in which art is practiced that we can keep relearning to recognize the intolerableness of conditions devoid of context—the quintessential quality of pornography. Space cleared and articulated by art reveals the obscenity of all forces of final consequence, all those conclusive triumphs that deflate the ego and put us to rest, all those routines which are but past conclusions extended in time. The resonant space

---

The bourgeois revolution was judicial. The proletarian revolution was economic. Ours will be cultural so that man can become himself.

—The Appeal from the Sorbonne

---

that art creates lets us realize that there is no *need* to be satisfied by the way things are, that so-called reality can be made to cry out for change.

Whenever we transform reality, we express our artistic impulse, our natural need to change desolating, disgusting, sickening, and finally deadly forces—evil situations—into life-giving ones. It is not that creative activity converts brute elements in nature and in man into objects of beauty but rather that our very action—not its end products—prevents us from becoming brutalized, from becoming dead objects, from ending. The artistic process itself—the treatment of everything seemingly completed as subject to reconstruction, reinterpretation, and review—humanizes us by enhancing our power to govern ourselves. It enables us to develop unfamiliar aspects of ourselves while freeing us to cope with the dehumanizing aspects of new conditions, new varieties of evil, exploitation, violence, brutality, and meanness.

Artistic processes—play, experiment, ongoing testing of self and others—are thus the very conditions of human survival. Making us conscious of recoverable self-sustaining resources within ourselves, they enable us to disrupt overpowering routines. Morse Peckham's words sum it up:

> The role of the artist demands that he offer violations of formal expectancies, that he offer occasions for the rehearsal of the endurance of cognitive tension. And the role of the perceiver demands that he search for such occasions and that he respond to them to the best of his ability. Artistic behavior, then, is not a pretty ornament to life but a terrible necessity which keeps man alive, aware, capable of perceiving that he is neither adequate nor inadequate to the demands of his environment but a perilous mixture of the two, capable of evading the sentimentalities of comedy and of tragedy. Art is the ingredient in human behavior which enables man to innovate, because it trains him to endure the cognitive tension which is the necessary preliminary to problem perception and genuine and meaningful innovation. To me, only such a psychological and biological explanation of artistic behavior can serve to make comprehensible the outpouring of energy, devotion, treasure and creativity at the feet of the terrible idol of art. Of all man's burdens, art is one of the most unendurable, and one of the most necessary. Deprived of it, he could not continue to be man.[9]

Time and space for play and art enable us to adapt and prevail. Thomas McGuane has the hero of *Ninety-Two in the Shade* observe that if you look life straight in the eye, it will kill you: "The great trick, contrary to the consensus of philosophy, is to avoid looking it straight in the eye. Everything askance and it all shines on."

6

Art as Political Action

If open space for politics, art, and play is the very ground for human survival, we are rightly concerned today with ways for enlarging it. How can we move out of the meager arenas to which self-expressive action is consigned by the Myth of Liberalism? Is it possible to overcome the frustrating, teasing politics of liberalism and inject more varied interests into our existence?

Oriented by the Myth of Liberalism, we tend to feel that we cannot possibly succeed in establishing ourselves politically until *after* we have accumulated the resources and acquired the appropriate expertise. We distinguish between means and ends and regretfully note that we are not yet prepared to live more rewarding lives. We also know, however, that on past occasions when we had seemed least prepared, we were nonetheless able to indulge in forms of play. We would remain in touch with a child or a lover by impersonating some hero or villain, when we felt secure, or even a flower unfolding or a bear growling. Vulnerable to being criticized as infantile and clumsy, we yet knew that in our transgression of approved behavior we had won a freedom to act that we would be foolish *ever* to relinquish. We would

---

In the beginning God and nature provided. Things were what they were. Adam and Eve, both of one flesh, were at peace with themselves and at home in the garden with its tree of life and its forbidden tree of the knowledge of good and evil. But beguiled by a serpent, Eve decided to ignore God's warning that eating fruit from the tree of knowledge—even touching the tree—would prove to be deadly. Rather than simply accepting things as they were, she hoped to be enlightened about them. Like God, she wanted to introduce distinctions, make judgments, establish some things as right and others as wrong. And of course she also got Adam involved. Clearly, theirs was a failure to trust in providence, a suspicion that the future could not be left to take care of itself. They felt it was necessary to plan ahead. And to do this sensibly they had to know which ends were really good and which ones really evil.

The results are familiar. The serpent, about whom not much has been said but a great deal repressed, was cursed and made to crawl on his belly. Adam and Eve did become duly enlightened, and of course so ashamed of parts of themselves that they quickly took pains to cover these with aprons of fig leaves. More followed. Initially of one flesh, Adam and Eve were placed in opposition to one another and man was assigned to rule over woman. The soil no longer yielded its fruit without causing man to sweat while tilling it. The feeling that time was suspended and life ever present disappeared as man —and woman—were expelled from the garden. The gate was guarded by an angel and the tree of life inside by a flaming sword.

Now and again, some prophet in our midst repeats this myth and proclaims it is time to slip past the angel and brave the flaming sword. Life in the garden is good, he says, and life outside is evil. We need to plan and organize and fight only one more time, doing only once more precisely what had led to our expulsion. As he exhorts us no one is there to remind him that the myth is ours, that we ourselves have drawn the line between the garden and the world outside, that every moment is a beginning, that we can always commence living where we happen to be, that we can treat ourselves and the ground underfoot as one even while giving comfort to the serpent.

---

in fact strain to prolong such moments of madness, wanting to keep our affair —if that is what it was—from ever having to end. In short, we know well enough how desirable and possible it is to suspend the means-ends distinction. And we can get further support by following anthropologists who enjoy reporting how other cultures manage to avoid every denouement. For the Balinese, as Clifford Geertz has observed,

social activities do not build, or are not permitted to build, toward definitive consummations. Quarrels appear and disappear, on occasion they even persist, but they hardly ever come to a head. Issues are not sharpened for decision, they are blunted and softened in the hope that the mere evolution of circumstances will resolve them, or better yet, that they will simply evaporate. Daily life consists of self-contained, nomadic encounters in which something either happens or does not—an intention is realized or it is not, a task accomplished or not. When the thing doesn't happen—the intention is frustrated, the task unaccomplished—the effort may be made again from the beginning at some other time; or it may simply be abandoned. Artistic performances start, go on (often for very extended periods when one does not attend continuously but drifts away and back, chatters for a while, sleeps for a while, watches rapt for a while), and stop; they are as uncentered as a parade, as directionless as a pageant. Ritual often seems, as in the temple celebrations, to consist largely of getting ready and cleaning up. . . . Even in such a dramatically more heightened ceremony as the Rangda Barong, fearful witch and foolish dragon combat ends in a state of complete irresolution, a mystical, metaphysical, and moral standoff leaving everything precisely as it was, and the observer—or anyway the foreign observer—with the feeling that something decisive was on the verge of happening but never did.

In short, events happen like holidays. They appear, vanish, and reappear—each discrete, sufficient unto itself, a particular manifestation of the fixed order of things. Social activities are separate performances; they do not march toward some destination, gather toward some denouement. As time is punctual, so life is. Not orderless, but qualitatively ordered, like the days themselves, into a limited number of established kinds. Balinese social life lacks climax because it takes place in a motionless present. . . .[1]

There is but one way to find out whether the Balinese life-style can be adopted elsewhere—by deliberate testing. We can discover how prepared we are for play and politics only by acting as if the ground for it actually existed

---

"The students," say the detractors of the May 1968 Movement, "don't really want revolution. They're quite content to play at it." I don't think all the students referred to here would totally reject this statement. A certain theatrical element was often present in the more serious as well as in lighter moments. To borrow a sociological vocabulary that is particularly well adapted to these circumstances, the social actors suddenly discovered that the author of the play in which they were acting had disappeared. Society had stopped handing out roles. Some of them, like wretched musicians suddenly without a score, took fright. Others chose to become their own authors.

—Alfred Willener

---

under our very feet, already ours and begging to be used. We would have to begin by treating each of our efforts to create political space not as a means to some future state but as an end, as itself political. This would entail allowing our very tactics to be expressive of our conflicting potentialities. *If we wish to reorganize space so that it will impel us to express our hidden selves, the process of reorganization itself must bring them out of hiding.* The only question is how much experience at any particular time we can openly bear to manage.

The risks and the agony of continuously responding to this question have been dramatized in the theater of Antonin Artaud. Forever breaking up his projects to allow for the entry of hidden possibilities, he did no more than to use the stage to display his consequent disappointments. He kept offering an endless series of dramatic fragments, all scrupulously designed to reveal his plays as failures and him as victim. He ceaselessly expressed his contempt for whatever *is*, for completed literature and definitive action. He worked toward a theater filled with nothing but his suffering—no sets, no props, no curtains. To the extent that he could continue to express his impulse in successive plays, he implicated actors and audiences, sharing the pain caused by his unresolvable quandary. Ultimately he was to attack *every* effort to reconcile conflicting interests. Transcending art and politics, his act became, like all despair, sheer egocentricity, a private incommunicable madness. It demonstrated how hard it is to acknowledge the perverse as normal and the weak as strong—and, further, how hard it is to remove the signposts in the spaces ahead which misleadingly tell us what is *really* perverse, weak, ugly, and therefore private.

Treating nothing sunk in the ground as rooted, Artaud risked acknowledging that we have but ourselves adrift in space and time of our making. He lets us infer that if we do wish to rely on forms and disciplines to keep us from being ravaged by despair, they must be suffused by nothing but that negative energy which, like the explosive potency of Gandhi's nonviolence, breaks the categories in our minds and the boundaries of our institutions. Our form of action cannot be allowed to define what the Myth of Liberalsim categorizes and closes off as "Society" or as "The Individual." Whatever we bring into the balance of our interests will then be derived not from some specified ideal ahead but from the barely reached poles of our own experience, from those primal forces which keep us alive and oscillating. We will then bring ourselves to life by calling on them, but letting none of them take over, by welcoming them, but only in the form of performances deliberately staged to keep us from ending.

To find oneself in such a politics—to locate one's very self in it—is to *keep* one's balance, to *manage* an endless "turning and turning in widening

---

It flies not directly whither it is bound, but advances by circles. . . . The poetry of motion. Not as preferring one place to another, but enjoying each as long as possible. . . . As if that hawk were made to be the symbol of my thought, how bravely he came around over those parts of the wood which he had not surveyed, taking in a new segment, annexing new territories!

—Henry David Thoreau

---

gyre." Remaining poised in a state of permanent anticipation, knowing the hopelessness of hoping for something known, we accept what so far has been regarded as peculiarly the lot of women, of whoever awaits improvement while knowing better, of whoever has learned how to pretend and prevaricate. This anticipatory posture is best understood as a precarious state of pure contingency; it is characteristic of those who resist the pressure to bring matters to an end at last. Such individuals are loyal to a state which is vacuous and insubstantial, literally pointless. They embrace a contradiction in terms, a radically disjunctive and unsettling foundation which openly proclaims that nothing is there, that an unknown, absent guest is brilliantly present.

The predicament is familiar: how can we take note of something without assuming it possesses qualities and boundaries? Clearly, we would have to make less than ideal the very terms by which we express our ideal. The language for constructing our models of reality would then be just as indeterminate—as untrustworthy, imprecise, indiscrete, unstable, restless, active—as the reality which the language is designed to comprehend. Our speech acts, as they have been aptly called, would keep alienating us from whatever they proclaim to be true. They would conclusively affirm only inconclusiveness. They would deny that point at the horizon where lines meet and end, where we falsely presume the truth to reside. Our performances, accordingly, could not be treated as finished works but as processes to keep us in relation.

We are understandably reluctant to enter an unbounded, indeterminate emptiness in which all is process. We are disoriented in the absence of fixed goals, or at least of milestones. Moreover, action which is not directed toward some objective seems morally indefensible: it is nothing other than play. And even if society could afford politics-as-play and play-as-end, so the argument goes, it would risk being taken over by its least scrupulous elements, by those who would opt for hell as their playground.

You say that my argument implies that any change is for the better. But that's not it. Of course, better does imply good, but "good" doesn't have to be anything real that we can talk about while we're alive. Why not simply favor change—not change "for the better," not change because change has instrumental value? You know to excess what happens when we make such a commitment to change: we give sadistic and masochistic opportunists the chance to exploit instabilities and impose a New Order. The cure? Not, I think, an Old Older but a more intense and sustained commitment to change—one so serious that it also justifies blocking those who mindlessly drive themselves and others toward destruction.

Yet is it not possible that a tyrannical society might really emerge—might in fact have been realized in the form of Hitler's regime—not because people engage in self-expressive action but because they are reacting to repressive, community-denying institutions which keep them from relating? If that is the case, our problem is how to enable people to relate. This clearly is not a problem on the agenda of liberalism. Time and space for relating, within the liberal order, remain private. When acting in public, the individual is to remain disconnected. He is to be kept from trusting others: mutual aid, as antitrust statutes proclaim, is conspiracy. Individuals are kept unrelated, wholly on their own, driven to bargain with others so as to make their isolated existence not less isolated but more abundantly sumptuous.

But what alternative is there to a state which blocks our communal feelings? What individual or social structure would free them? In its most radical form, the alternative state is necessarily so formless as to be incomprehensible. It can have no identifiable objective from which to derive an identifiable structure. It would be experienced—though not known—as that state of pure Nothing which Hegel identified with pure Being. He envisaged it as

> the aimless fickleness and instability of going to and fro, hither and thither, from one extreme of the self-same self-consciousness to the other contingent, confused and confusing consciousness. It does not itself bring these two thoughts of itself together. It finds its freedom, at one time, in the form of elevation above all the whirling complexity and all the contingency of mere existence, and again, at another time, likewise confesses to falling back upon what is unessential, and to being taken up with that. It lets the unessential content in its thought vanish; but in that very act *it is the consciousness of something unessential*. It announces absolute disappearance but the announcement *is*, and this consciousness is the evanescence expressly announced. It announces the nullity of seeing, hearing, and so on, yet *itself* sees and hears. . . .[2]

It is an aimless dynamism that Hegel would have us establish, insisting on nothing more than our sustained consciousness of it. It is a state of perpetual tension and infinite variability, possessed of no durable substance, primed to dissolve whatever habits and institutions might impose order and direction. Our consciousness of this state necessarily includes our knowledge of the past as it had once been—a seemingly impermeable presence that had excluded all options and thereby arrested the development of those implicated in it. In our new state of being, past afflictions have been transformed. Our health has become an assertive process—silent testimony to the range of transcended pain.

This view of the healthy body politic, I realize, may strike us as pathetically insubstantial. If its emptiness calls anything to mind, it is an image of "negative" men—nonheroes without qualities, picaresque drifters, hollow dissemblers. We are scarcely attracted. One of Henry James's characters, Lord Mellifont, defines our distaste:

> He directed the conversation by gestures as irresistible as they were vague; one felt as if without him it wouldn't have had anything to call a tone. This was essentially what he contributed to any occasion—what he contributed above all to English

public life. He pervaded it, he coloured it, he embellished it, and without him it would have lacked, comparatively speaking, a vocabulary. Certainly it wouldn't have had a style, for a style was what it had in having Lord Mellifont. He *was* a style.[3]

It is hard to overcome one's ambivalence toward the case for pure style (James himself added that, in whatever place Mellifont had been, "the place was utterly empty . . . he had ceased to be"). It is easy to have mixed feelings about men who amount to nothing, about what Robert Jay Lifton has described as protean man who conducts "an interminable series of experiments and exploration, some shallow, some profound, each of which can readily be abandoned in favor of still new psychological quests."[4] Lifton's studies of people in crisis have made especially clear how desperately one wants to reintroduce some firm nucleus, some secure essences of human nature. If Henry James indulged in no such hankering, perhaps he felt none after he created a net of relationships so elaborate that it holds even the most weightless of his characters, a net that gives his critics evidence, but no justification, for complaining about the absence of qualities which *matter*.

To accept a society of open-ended individuals requires acknowledging that nothing can give us significance save qualities which others attribute to us or which we can succeed in making others attribute to us. Only by acting in society can we give ourselves an air of reality. Thus it is only through relationships that individual lives acquire meaning. In the absence of relationships, we have no character, no essential nature. Of course, we can appear to be someone: we can display characteristics which appear to be real. Our masks can make us seem to be *really* affable or impudent, black or white, little or big, clean or dirty. But these characteristics are merely attributed. Functions of our relationships, they say nothing about our being, about "who we really are."

It is precisely this pure potentiality—the ineradicable truth that nothing is there as long as nothing has appeared—that I believe it imperative to acknowledge and affirm. Were an institutional order to allow us to come to terms with our essential emptiness, we would stop searching for our true identity. And we would be buoyed by the knowledge that we can bear the loss of not being someone. To sustain this posture is to surrender every definitive ideal—not only every final model of man and society but the very idea of a model defining human functions. We cannot permit our life lines to converge on some horizon. Our end, after all, is not to "get it all together," or to discover our true identity, or to find out who we *really* are. It is to engage in activities that keep breaking these very expectations, that keep violating familiar plots, sequences, and roles.

Such activities—our only ends—cannot be interpreted as preludes to harmony:

Existence has no goal or end; any comprehensive unity in the plurality of events is lacking. . . . One simply lacks any reason for convincing oneself that there is a *true*

world. Briefly: the categories "aim," "unity," "being" which we used to project
some value into the world looks valueless.[5]

Sheltered by the metaphysics of liberalism, we are disquieted by these words
of Nietzsche's. We wish to overcome the tensions of history and resolve our
contradictions. Yet the alternative to hedging and shifting is to move toward
some singular purity in which man as a being with self-knowledge—as
capable of watching himself and communicating what he sees—is extin-
guished. If we are to save our contradictory selves we have no choice but to
assume that our end is inherent in our action and that our action is split and
flawed at its very center. For us, Antigone and Creon must both be present
—present in the work which integrates them and beyond which stretches an
irreducible void.

Nietzsche is clearly the most commanding exponent of this postliberal
metaphysics. At the same time, he realized that Romantic movements would
be recurrently threatened by their progeny, half-hearted, immature Romantics
who would betray Romanticism by searching for a secure place to rest.
Therefore Nietzsche, as Morse Peckham has noted, could accept nothing but
a continuous transvaluation of values as a positive good:

> If . . . one accepted the fact that there was no ground, that there was no justification
> for the search for order and meaning and value, that the world was quite
> meaningless, quite without value, in both subject and object—for subject and
> object are one—then sorrow could be converted to joy. Eternal recurrence was the
> answer, continuous renewal of identity by continuous transformation and trans-
> valuation of style in art, in thought, and in individuality. Nietzsche realized that
> this is neither a world which once held value nor a world which holds without
> order, without meaning. The world is nothing. Value and identity are the ultimate
> illusions. We emerge from nothingness and encounter the nothingness of the
> world, and in so doing we create being. But being can be renewed only if we
> recognize that being is illusion. With that recognition as our ultimate weapon we
> can re-create it, not from sorrow but from joy. From the desire for value we create
> ourselves, but to renew that value we must destroy ourselves. The profoundest
> satisfaction of the human mind is the creation of the world—out of nothingness.
> From that act of creation emerges the *sense* of value, the *sense* of identity, which
> are sources of joy only if we recognize them as illusions. The sense of order, the
> sense of meaning, and the sense of identity are but instruments for the act of
> creation. Thus the Romantic once more enters into history and human life, for to
> create is to choose, without ever knowing whether or not the choice is the right
> choice, for the act of choice changes the world. And so we can never know, even
> by hindsight, whether or not we chose rightly, for the situation in which we
> performed the act of creation and choice no longer exists. And this solves the
> problem of re-entry, for it is clear that alienation is the illusion of the Romantic.

And so Nietzsche's work is the triumph of Romanticism, for he solved its
problem of value and returned the Romantic to history, by showing that there is no
ground to value and that there is no escape from history. As the Romantic had
always known but had never, until Nietzsche, been able to believe, reality is
history, and only the experience of reality has value, an experience to be achieved

by creating illusions so that we may live and by destroying them so that we may recover our freedom. Value is process, a perpetual weaving and unweaving of our own identities. Sorrow is a sentimental lust for finality; joy is the penetration beyond that sentimentality into the valuelessness of reality, into its freedom, the achievement of which is inevitably its loss. Joy is the eternal recurrence of the same problem, forever solved and forever unsolvable. Nietzsche found what the Romantic had sought for a hundred years, a way of encompassing, without loss of tension, the contrarieties and paradoxes of human experience. The *feel* of reality, in the subject is tension and the sense of contradiction. As for violating others, that is the ultimate moral responsibility, for to maintain the tension of human experience, which is to achieve and destroy and re-achieve value, we must violate others—as we must violate ourselves.[6]

There would seem to be no way to keep that inner voice of ours from asking why one should, after all, seek to "maintain the tension of human experience." What *good* is it? Why assume the agony of expressing one's potentialities? No answer to this question has ever been immune to attack by critics who insist that the mere fact of man's inclination to express himself surely cannot justify any *specific* form of self-expression. They point out that a good number of expressive acts are actually demeaning, destructive, and deadly. Lacking vision or generosity, the individual turns out to act destructively. He will refuse to express some of his potentialities and deny other people the opportunity to express theirs. It is best to admit this, and yet to add that basically, beneath all destructive action there remains the disposition to relate man's impulses. The urge to keep relating to a progressively larger realm of life is more fundamental then any *specific* end to which one might aspire. Implicit in each of our actions is a claim that remains utterly undeniable, *for every denial is itself an attempt to reach others who might give our denial a hearing.* Expressed denial to relate is itself an effort to relate. Even suicidal acts are efforts to signal, to let others know about one's fate. At bottom, every specific claim in favor of some course of action—however deplorable the action because it would narrow one's life—implicitly affirms our more general, if unspoken claim that we are alive and deserve a hearing. Whatever end we may claim to desire, our claim also constitutes an affirmation of our social self, an appeal to others, an effort to hold an audience, to relate to a community.

In different words, I would pretend to no justification for self-expressive action as such. All I would offer the critics of this view (assuming they sought my response) is the evidence that all of us are inexplicably determined to affirm as much of ourselves as we can. Ours is an irreducible, incommensurable striving to participate in the whole of creation by expressing the manifold possibilities of our being. And it is this disposition to know ourselves in action that I would regard quite simply as the way it is, as The Way, as *wholly* natural.

As I have already admitted, our nature may not always be in evidence. It may have sunk out of sight. It may have been deformed and repressed. Having felt bored or perhaps terrorized, we may have wanted to catch our breath and sort things out. We may then have fallen in with the polished rationalism of Aristotle and divided the universe, our work, and ourselves into classes and subclasses. And confusing the parts with the whole, we may finally have gone on to eliminate entire populations just to preserve one of the parts, just to make certain that the world will be virtuous, or white, or skilled, or normal. In the process we may have enlisted priests, teachers, and experts in violence to help us promote "responsible" conduct, "good" works, and "high" culture. In short, we may have become pervasively destructive—and then drawn from our past the false conclusion that man's tendency to destructiveness is his true nature, that civilization therefore demands the repression of what comes naturally.

The problem, however, is not how to control our nature in the name of some higher good but how to institutionalize the procedures for avoiding the destruction of ourselves and our environment, how to stop confusing parts with the whole, how to stop assuming that God and Virtue are on one side and not on any other. But how can we institutionalize the endless conflict generated by man's striving to express himself? What public order—what *politics*—can enable us to feel free to bring our potentialities into the open where they will be acclaimed for adding new dimensions to the world and appreciated for reducing that boredom and anxiety which lead people in the first place to express themselves in destructive ways?

You raise a tough, probably unanswerable question when you wonder how my alternative model might be embodied in specifically political forms and how a political community might arise from the self-expressive activity of individuals. You want an answer to my rhetorical questions. I'm in trouble, and I know it. I simply can't specify the language allowing me to express what it feels like to live without the distinction between subject and predicate, actor and action, theory and practice, dancer and dance. And I don't think that my blaming the lack of language is any more a cop-out on my part than the insistent silences of Nietzsche, Wittgenstein, and Marx. I suppose I could speak in parables, but given the quality of my diction (as opposed to Beckett's, Nietzsche's, Borges's, or Kafka's), I may as well remain at rest—or perhaps inject this paragraph into my manuscript.

The way to proceed, it should now be possible to recall, is indicated by my didactic model of the performances of the artist. The aesthetics of Romanticism clarifies how every particular element of the artist's work constitutes at once the occasion and the impetus for expressive action. His work is a usable

model for us insofar as it treats spectators as potentially creative, underdeveloped artists. It carefully leads them to follow his steps, to imitate his
performance. In what is a series of *political* acts, he makes their eyes follow
his recorded lines. Moved to come into touch with their uncomprehended
experiences, his spectators in the end become confident about their own
powers of comprehension, of controlling themselves, and finally of experi-
menting with designing their own structures, their own history. Jack
Nicholson's portrait of McMurphy in "One Flew over the Cuckoo's Nest"
(1975) reveals how an energetic actor can succeed in galvanizing even the
most apathetic characters. Reviewing one of Pinter's plays, Stanley Kauffmann has described the initial part of this process:

> Pinter's playwriting can be seen as . . . dealing with well-defined objects
> arranged in such a way that the point is not in their detail—the fine details are in a
> way deliberate deception—but in the trajectory outlined by the way they are
> deployed, in the space they enclose, in the surprise and shock and laughter that the
> succession of these details arouses in us.
> In this view the *audience* writes the play (as the audience writes Cage's music)
> within boundaries described by the author and in response to data and stimuli that
> he supplies. The pauses and silences specified in Pinter's scripts are not only
> musical similes, they are opportunities to "catch up"; the play rests for a moment
> while you draw abreast of it in simultaneous creation.[7]

A full-scale case in point was provided in 1972 by Cornell University's art
museum in the form of Norman Daly's construction and display, "The
Civilization of Llhuros: An Exhibition of Artifacts and Recent Excavation of
Vanibo, Houndee, Draikum, and Other Sites." Nothing whatever was
known about the Llhuros culture until Daly created it, invented scholarly
sources to confirm his creation, provided an *errata* sheet as if his fictions
were truths, and moved the New York State Council on the Arts to support
his project. What he furnished in the end was but the beginning for others, for
museum visitors who entered his world and found themselves impelled to act
in order to relate familiar objects within an unfamiliar context.

There is in principle no difference between Daly's exhibit and Joyce's
Finnegans Wake or Arno Schmidt's endlessly translatable *Die Schule der
Atheisten*, an intricate amalgam published in 1972 which projects past literary
forms onto a future setting, its very typography an obstacle course, a design to
keep from ending, a circular track allowing no firm conclusion other than that
the work has continuous being in time. Similarly, Marcel Duchamp's lifelong
project was to keep the man-made world from being seen as an accumulation
of end products. He deprived commercial objects—such "ready-mades" as a
bicycle wheel—of their finality, making their ambiguity apparent by placing
them on pedestals. Labeling them Art Objects and freeing others to accept the
status he bestowed on them, he loosened up his environment. But finally he
gave up—or succeeded—completely and determined to leave nothing
objective to frame and display, to keep everything open, to postpone all ends.

"Use 'delay' instead of picture," he wrote in 1923 on a memo meant to accompany "Large Glass," a construction of his he abandoned after bringing it to a state of "definitive completion." Communication, if it was to occur at all, was possible only through his fine-spun transparencies, through his endless series of frauds, deceptions, parodies, and distractions.

Without explicitly noting how one's very life may be an act of political leadership as well as a work of art that turns spectators into actors, Harold Rosenberg has nevertheless made it possible to see the authority-destructive, egalitarian thrust of Duchamp's career. Existing, as Rosenberg says, *only in the mirror of what was said about him*, Duchamp encouraged public opinion to create him. His productions, interviews, disguises, performances, and pronouncements were designed to impel spectators to invest his enigmas with meaning and thereby to construct reality for themselves. Because the image in the mirror was ultimately to be attacked by the defenders of established culture, Duchamp's posture has become more clear. The case *against* him, summed up by Rosenberg, can actually serve to make his great act pervasively appealing.

(1) He is held responsible for leading art off the track of evolutionary advance. . . . Instead of extending the formal potentialities of the Cézanne-Cubist tradition, he deviated into eccentricity. . . . He has boasted that he has no use for "good" painting, he has fought against taste, good and bad, and in a message to Alfred Stieglitz he expressed the desire to see people "despise painting." Thus despite the apologetics of his supporters, he is fundamentally anti-art and a practitioner of aesthetic nihilism. . . .

(2) He has built up the importance of the artist's signature at the expense of his product. . . . [He has] brought about the degradation of the art object (Warhol), and even its total elimination (Conceptual art). In the Duchamp era, one can exhibit one's own body as a "work of art" or make a record of one's temperature or blood pressure as "information" equivalent to a painting.

(3) In adopting the ready-made, Duchamp has introduced the deadly rival of artistic creation—an object fabricated by machine and available everywhere, an object chosen, as he put it, on the basis of pure "visual indifference," in order to "reduce the ideal of aesthetic consideration to the choice of the mind, not to the ability or cleverness of the hand." In the world of the ready-made, anything can become a work of art through being signed by an artist. All particular genres and disciplines become superfluous. The title "artist," no longer conferred in recognition of skill in conception and execution, is achieved by means of publicity.

(4) Duchamp has placed innovative art under permanent suspicion of being a hoax. . . . Were the bicycle wheel mounted on a stool, the snow shovel, the dog comb inscribed with "a nonsensical phrase" to be taken seriously as works of art?—especially after the artist had supplied a description of "the characteristics of a true ready-made: no beauty, no ugliness, nothing particularly aesthetic about it."[8]

Duchamp's self-conscious posturing may be seen to constitute an affirmation of equality: it opposes judgments of taste, praises performance over end result, deflates Art and the title Artist, and finally assaults the very ideas of professionalism and integrity. "Would it have been possible," Rosenberg inquires,"for him to refuse to be photographed playing chess with a naked girl?" And if Duchamp could play at *everything*—if he could convert his

---

Choice and taste can only be considered neurotic.

—Les Levine

---

scandals into successes—so can everyone. If he could waste his time, others need not hoard theirs. Revealing that there is no self to falsify, he frees others from guilt. Why should anyone feel obliged to live up to pretensions not of his own making?

We continue to be blind to the distinctively political character of such de-creative activities so long as we see the organization of paintings, poems, symphonies, or plays as somehow different from the organization of legislative, judicial, or bureaucratic arenas. Were we to treat every organization of life that invites the participation of our various interests as a work of art, a new standard for judging could emerge. We would have to regard activities as rational and efficient precisely insofar as they maximize participation and multiply relationships. We would then perceive the irrationality and inefficiency of predefined margins and unambiguous centers, firm boundaries and secure structures. We would question closed admissions and penalized departures. We would doubt the usefulness of predefined ends which justify the calculation of economical means, which demand specialization and hierarchy, clocked time and squared space, policy analysis distinct from policy execution, administration distinct from politics, outputs distinct from inputs. And if we were to act on the basis of our new perceptions, we would come to know art without artists, politics without politicians, therapy without therapists, science without scientists, love without lovers, life without heroes. We would all be merely acting. As our nouns would ineluctably turn into verbs, as we would at last not mind surrendering our monumental hopes, we would move beyond capitalized Good and Evil.

The place to begin can only be close to home where one's action can have practical effects. Yet I realize this is also the place where we are intimidated and preoccupied by our daily routines. We're frozen, blame "the times," and observe they are "not ripe." But perhaps we can accelerate the times by being unassuming in our plans. We might content ourselves to do no more than make quite familiar experiences more apparent to ourselves, identify what seem but little troubles—the seemingly trivial disruptions and embarrassments in our ordinary existence. We can take note of their underlying context until we see, for example, that a child "making a scene" is doing precisely that, and is "out of control" only from the parents' view. Or we can see that a riot is not just men-running-amok but more basically people creating a form for getting recognition. As we recognize others—as in fact we recognize riotous elements within ourselves—we *give* them recognition. We identify them more fully than they identify themselves. By such acts, we do not hold the mirror up to them but rather exaggerate and dramatize and publicize what they appear to say.

In short, we can take more full account of what is repressed within the liberal order and within ourselves at every moment. *The very process of making repressed interests public will constitute the alternative beyond liberalism.* Engaging in self-disclosing acts, we do not hope for the day when we will *finally* enter the postliberal world: we assume instead that the postliberal world is buried in the present and that its realization is achieved in every move to express it. Thus its contours are defined not by some blueprint

---

It is a question of denying the Germans an instant of illusion or resignation. The burden must be made still more irksome by awakening a consciousness of it, and shame must be made more shameful still by rendering it public. Every sphere of German society must be depicted as the partie honteuse *of German society; and these petrified social conditions must be made to dance by singing their own melody to them. The nation must be taught to be* terrified *of itself, in order to give it* courage.

—Karl Marx

---

for utopia but by increasingly penetrating pictures of both prevailing institutions and our current images of them.

Were we to engage in such action we would deny ourselves all plans for the future. We would be satisfied with an image of a society disposed to keep its members in circulation by integrating states of being which have become hardened because not brought in relation to their opposites. Oriented by this image, we would treat even the most fanatical acts as disguises, as evidence of the determination of women and men to express themselves in as many guises as they can afford. We would give recognition to the weak, disreputable parts of our lives and bring them into the existing balance of interests. We would become more discursive and playful, certainly less fully punctuated than my sentences, but just as questionable.

Part Three

Implementing a Political Aesthetics

"I'm still looking," she said. "Someone sure of himself."

"Jim was like that. He used to have lots of drive. Hot for certainties. Knew where he was headed and knew what was right. Worked on himself and straightened out the company. Kept working on me too. Always judging and doing things. Lots of excitement, but hard to take. Of course, he still knows what's right, but he's no longer sure. All the energy and toughness have gone out of him. Easier to live with though."

"But I'm looking for someone who's not judgmental at all."

"Sure—someone loose, easy, casual, nonchalant. Lets things go, drifts. But he'd still have one thing in common with Jim: no energy."

"Well, yes, but he'd be comfortable. Easy to live with."

"A bore."

"All right then—let's make up someone who takes everything as it comes but with energy."

"He wouldn't just take things as they come—he'd make them come."

"A real turn-on."

7

Directives for Action

The politics of liberalism brings out some of man's least attractive traits first by splitting the individual from society, private life from public life, and the means to achieve ends from the ends themselves, and then by keeping the separated entities in a frozen state. I have been discussing works of art because they can serve as models to loosen up the frozen polarities of liberalism. The artistic ventures to which I have referred legitimate action as a self-sufficient end. Ideally they induce everyone participating in such action —foremost the artist—to develop himself under various guises without ever treating any one of the roles he plays as terminal. He is to remain free not merely to act but to remain in action. He is ultimately to possess nothing whatever other than his consciousness of his freedom.

The risks of adhering to this orientation have been widely publicized. Confronting nothing but an open, empty future, people are said to become disconcerted. In quest of objectives but finding none, they are unable to move at all or else move only in a state of hysterical frenzy. They then crave stabilizing rituals. They yearn for myths in which they can implicitly believe and to which they can submit. Finding purposeless games to be intolerable, they will cling to any purpose just to bring them back to their senses. Are people not rightly given pause by contemporary events which occurred precisely because cruel men believed in nothing while their victims lacked the conviction to engage in resistance? Empty public spaces would seem to invite a holocaust. Free time for gratuitous acts—acts literally uncalled for—reveals only how brutalized we can all become. Was not Hitler's regime truly uncalled for, nothing but a self-validating convulsion, a direct outpouring of naked power? Was not the Vietnam War—the American case in point—an *empty* show of power, a war waged (as is shown by Robert Jay Lifton's record of its American veterans) only for *counterfeit* purposes?

The men described experiencing *themselves* as counterfeit. They spoke of having been "like boys playing soldiers"—of having the feeling upon entering combat: "God, this is right out of a movie!" One said simply: "Nothing was real." The game of war, they seemed to be saying, was there, but reduced to childish deception and self-deception. The play element was isolated, disconnected, never a part of a believable ritual or contest. They were counterfeit warriors engaging in counterfeit play.[1]

If we should actually come to believe that an aesthetics of destruction and deception is good, how can we regard the phenomenon of Vietnam as bad?

> "It's only a game. I've only been pretending to be irresponsible."
> "Pretending? You are irresponsible. You do just as you like."
> "But I'm playing with others."
> "You keep them in mind?"
> "That's what makes it so hard. But the worst part is when people playing with me can't keep others in mind and don't want to play."

Surely nothing about America's spectacular performance in an Asian theater of operation was real, and nothing said about it could be believed in. Didn't the Vietnam War, as Lifton claims, make manifest America's hidden potential for the destruction of authenticity? It would seem to have been an elaborate, virtually interminable performance rather than a meaningful, goal-oriented project:

> From the atrocity-producing situation in Vietnam; to the military-political arrangements responsible for it; to the system of law confronted by militant opponents of the war; to the pre-existing but war-exacerbated antagonisms around race, class, ethnicity, and age; to the war-linked economic recession; to collusion in the war's corruption by virtually all of the professions and occupations—what is there left that we can call authentic?[2]

Using Vietnam to provide an image of America as counterfeit, Lifton implies that because empty, pointless games amount to the collapse of all that is human, it is time for Americans to recover, to inquire "what is left that they can call authentic." It is time to identify a meaningful purpose once again, to shape up and get at the *real* truth at last so as to fulfill America's *genuine* mission.

Yet if inhuman behavior inheres not in the unreality or absurdity of the world but rather in our inability to *sustain* the unreality and absurdity, would we not reject missions precisely because they are purposeful, heroic, and authentic? We might recall that it was the American effort to reach its objective which served to justify the relentless movement to grind men down, to numb, mutilate, and waste them, to make them into one-dimensional, survival-craving mechanisms. That is, to realize an objective, men were systematically privatized, deprived of the opportunity to play the game. For the Americans whom Lifton quotes—none of them high-ranking officers who in fact were buoyed by the opportunity for action—the war was clearly *not* some game. It was for real, terribly authentic, a matter of survival and death. There were drugs to help out—but little of that truly playful, hopeless spirit expressed by one briefing officer: "*I* don't know why *I'm* here. *You* don't know why *you're* here. But since we're *both* here, we might as well try to do a good job and do our best to stay alive." Lifton rightly notes that this playful posture reflects the lack of authentic purpose, and he candidly adds that it does insert "a modicum of out-front honesty into the situation's basic absurdity, so that the absurdity itself can become shared," so that it can become a basis for "cooperation, brotherhood, and mutual love. . . ."[3] Nevertheless, Lifton can't accept this unheroic posture: it clearly lacks idealism. He senses no promise in the *shared* recognition of life's pointlessness, in a *community* that comes into being when all are free to play (as only a military elite was in Vietnam), to play games devoid of consequences for *any* participants. He still wants something definitively real. For the unheroic game proposed by the briefing officer he would substitute action made authentic because guided by an authentic purpose.[4]

Lifton may be right: men cannot always manage to govern themselves without the illusion that their lives have some true center, some ultimate goal beyond doubt. Perhaps a shared concern for our survival—the survival of *all* our capacities—is insufficient to temper us. To keep ourselves from surrendering our humanity, we may need (as Lifton implies) some true faith, some belief in immortality, some benign church, and some nocturnal council. Had the illusory dualities and absolutes embodied in the Myth of Liberalism been duly upheld they might in fact have restrained Americans in Vietnam (as they might have saved Germany in the 1930s). John Locke's right reason plus the United States Constitution strictly interpreted might have stopped the war Americans imposed on others and themselves. Conceivably, then, the Myth of Liberalism is not wholly useless. Those with the bearing of, say, Chief Justice Charles Evans Hughes can still remind men in power that liberalism guarantees due process, that it assures the ultimate triumph of justice in Harlem, Selma, or Trenton, in quieter but no less lethal places, in a ward of Bellevue, a bituminous coal mine in West Virginia, a martial court at Schofield Barracks, a stockholders' meeting of General Electric, a living room off Central Park South. In such places, the Liberal Myth may even today hold overbearing men in check. And a look beyond American boundaries may make the Myth of Liberalism more attractive yet: its mere relics would embarrass the elites of Prague, Brasilia, or Cape Town. There are still innumerable places where it may be premature—as Lifton intimates—to move beyond liberalism and dispense with its authority.

Whenever adherence to the due process of liberalism can be *shown* to reduce victimization, projects undermining liberalism would seem to be misguided. Yet its defenders would have to show that fewer people would be victims—nonplayers—when action is *not* oriented by a sense of mission and purpose. The fears of liberals to the contrary, awareness of the ambiguity and inconsequence of action does not invariably lead to the surrender of civility. Even in extreme situations where men all but betray themselves, even in Vietnam, there are those who keep their temper and preserve their humanity by *sharing* their sense of futility.

At a minimum, a readiness to keep testing our capacity to live without hope and purpose may free men to become more candid about the harm they inflict when they *do* have hope and act under the banner of authority. They can at least take account of the officially organized violence done to groups certified to be *really* evil—women classified as "witches," children as "hyperactive," leaders as "indispensable," or novelists as "lackeys of the imperialist aggressor." Realizing that nature attaches none of these labels, they may become more free to identify and challenge the authorities who do the labeling. And they may then learn to what extent they can actually afford to dispense with given definitions of themselves and their institutions, perceiving how much time and space they actually have for the nonauthoritative, nonteleological, open-ended structures within themselves, within their space and their time.

Instructed to believe "there really isn't enough time" or "this really isn't the right place," we are shielded from the knowledge that reality may be appropriated by us. We remain arrested because we let ordinary language make absolutes of time and space. Captives of theory and committed to splitting theory from practice, we fail to enlarge our existence. Yet it remains possible to act even in situations which seem to offer no options. Condemned to a task that was real, Sisyphus (as Camus saw him) could still will himself to become conscious of his condition. Making the most of what little time and space he was allowed, he determined to display himself, to express what freedom he had as self-determined actor. Like the briefing officer quoted by Lifton, Sisyphus assumed no externally given purpose and defined his own. His game was no different in principle from any of the serious games we choose to play: it had no purpose beyond itself, no higher end, no telos. It merely expressed his consciousness in the face of forces threatening to extinguish it. The end inhered in the exercise of his will—not in Nature, History, Reality, or whatever abstractions elites invent to keep the powerless from acting.

Precisely how much—how little—usable time and space we actually have can be determined only by specific efforts to find out in practice. These entail probing so-called reality whenever and wherever we happen to have sufficient strength to stimulate ourselves and our environment. And we can do this only where we are—at home, at work, at play. It is pathetic to direct our attention —usually our after-dinner talk—to some distant system we are powerless to affect. Only where we actually have the power to interrogate dormant interests can we call them into being. Only where we are in actual touch with them can we affirm that they are not yet dead and not quite out of bounds, that they are still related to us *and all right*, that they might respond, acquire a presence of their own, and help keep us alive as well.

Projects that arouse and establish dormant interests cannot help but bridge the liberal gap between public and private concerns. Such projects will induce us to present ourselves in public, to speak when we have been mute, to act when we have been listless. They conform to the dictates of Romanticism: depart from secure settings; multiply aspects of yourself; risk becoming notorious as deserter, actor, criminal; break careers, commitments, and marriages whose futures remain locked in their pasts; bring atrophied private elements into your conscious life.

To respond to these imperatives is to question the myth of a hard and fast social reality, one part *really* private and the other *really* public. Yet questioning the existing compartments of society, we keep courting vertigo. The problem is how, in practice, to *keep* courting it. On the one hand, we need to escape the boredom and anxiety which grow in privacy. On the other, we need secure public stages on which our lives may be extended, common ground for continuous collective action. The practical difficulty is that no one can say whether any existing stage is too open to those whose zeal to enter and act would destroy it or too closed to make the action enticing. There is no theory which can inform us that an actual stage provides a proper balance—apart from the exasperatingly circular theory which holds that something does not lean too much one way when it does not lean too much the other. Consequently we can ascertain the extent to which our stages for action are excessively open or excessively confining only by trial and error, only in the process of complicating and endangering our lives. *What* really constitutes and circumscribes a well-balanced household, law firm, research laboratory, athletic arena, old people's home, newspaper office, medical clinic, workshop, prison compound, or university campus—*any* theater of operations—is simply not specifiable in the abstract, in theory divorced from action.

The answer to what precisely is well-balanced and "rational" must depend on experimental action. Once we stop appreciating existing social structures

The intellectual content of any rational activity forms neither a single logical system, nor a temporal sequence of such systems. Rather, it is an intellectual enterprise whose "rationality" lies in the procedures governing its historical development and evolution. For certain limited purposes, we may find it useful to represent the provisional outcome of such an enterprise in the form of a "propositional system," but this will remain an abstraction. The system so arrived at is not the primary reality; like the notion of a geometrical point, it will be a fiction or artifact of our own making. In all our subsequent enquiries, therefore, our starting-point will be the living, historically-developing intellectual enterprises within which concepts find their collective use; and our results must be referred back for validation to our experience in those historical enterprises. . . .

We must begin, therefore, by recognizing that rationality is an attribute, not of logical or conceptual systems as such, but of the human activities or enterprises of which particular sets of concepts are the temporary, cross-sections: specifically of the procedures by which concepts, judgments, and formal systems currently accepted in those enterprises are criticized and changed.

—Stephen Toulmin

because they conform to some Real Structure located in Absolute Space, we are free to treat them as open to testing. They are not yet final and promise further contradictions and variation, more in the way of suspense, climax, and drama.

Some of the procedures for moving toward this ideal have been spelled out by Orion White. A student of public administration, he has inquired how one might encourage organizations to grow by enabling them to discover—and respond to—the contradictions they harbor. He urges that the professional seeking to change an organization would ideally

work from an informal (even sect-like) network with as low a visibility as possible so that there would be little opportunity for him to be defined as possessing ordinary professional motives. He would not make claims that he could make things "better" in organizations for the further development and propagation of his change ideology. . . . He would necessarily operate *within* existing institutions and not threaten them. That is, a change agent would hold conventional organizational posts (e.g., personnel officer in a public agency, university professor, consultant in a firm, middle manager in a corporation, etc.) and would seek to facilitate the types of role adjustment changes which have been typical of organization change efforts since the field of management and administration began. He would seek only through serendipitous opportunities afforded from this conventional post to bring about change toward a true dialectical organization. . . . There would be no gratuitously offered claim that the dialectical organization is a "solution" to a problematic status quo. No claim would be made to superior psychological health, and no utopia would be offered. . . .

A second aspect of the change strategy is that the change agent would take as his objective simply to facilitate the individual's conversion of [unexpressed] psychic energy—no more. This means that, working through his conventional role, he would attempt to develop a base of legitimacy—mainly a personal relationship— with the leadership of the organization—and then set about to discover those few in the organization who in the natural course of their lives are coming into confrontation with unconscious psychic forces and are finding themselves hindered in dealing with these because of the constraints of their organizational role. This organizational impingement might be affecting either the professional or the personal sphere of the person's life. Either area would be legitimate territory for the concern of the change agent. What the change agent would do after discovering these people is to act as a *mediator* between these people and those in the organization who represent the role constraints which are hindering their psychic development. The objective of this mediational effort would not be change in attitude or philosophy as much as it would be to negotiate *structural alternatives for the individual* that better fit his current psychic condition. . . .

An illustration of what this means can be drawn from the case of women. One of the major efforts of the current movement is to raise the consciousness of women—in somewhat the same sense that this term is being discussed here. Some women are finding that as they do this and their consciousness changes, so does the pattern of their life-style—or at least a desire for a different life-style emerges in them. One significant innovation in this regard is the desire of women to live together communally or in pairs and raise children without husbands. One may raise questions as to the desirability of this change, but what is relevant here is only that the evolution of the female's consciousness apparently requires this from *her* point of view. A mediator's interest, upon discovering such a woman in an organization where he is engaged, would be in seeing how to facilitate this change by negotiating a role for her in the organization which is compatible with the psychic revolution that is occurring within her. This means in the case of many women who are doing this at present that they will wish to share a job—that is, for two women (who are living together) to take a single job, and for each to fulfill one half of a meaningful work life, and a life with their children at home. . . . One could imagine that in many cases there would be no actual *technical* limits on allowing women to do this. There would like as not, however, be many attitudinal obstacles to the scheme on the part of the leadership of the organization, since this idea would violate the conventional normative order upon which the organization is based. What the mediator would do is attempt to negotiate some mutually acceptable definition of the role for the women in the organization—a role definition which as much as possible met the concerns of the organizational leadership *and* the women concerned.

As role renegotiations such as this occurred in the organization, it would no doubt stimulate the psychic development of others, as they saw real possibilities for a more compatible joining of their psychological life with their work life. Hence the process would continue until, probably, the organization's structure would itself become a process, constantly in flux, but firmly, realistically, and rationally rooted in the psychic needs of the individuals of which the organization is constituted. After a point, the process of structural negotiation could move to the group level of team building and then to the organization as a whole, where the organization would become in effect a community of individuals with its own "reality". . . .[5]

An elaborate metaphor revealing how it is possible to follow White's program and continuously incorporate new aspects of experience in our lives is provided by Luke Rinehart's *The Diceman* (1971)—a somewhat lumpish novel, a magnificent idea. Whenever the narrator's last specific project becomes boring, he decides to give himself six alternative roles to play, masks to wear, courses to take—each barely thinkable and feasible—and then promises himself to abide by the throw of his die. Of course, when up against it he may be reluctant to take the actual course the die has specified (guilt, shame, pride, inertia, anxiety, or good taste keep intervening). But fortunately he remembers his boredom and is even more reluctant to break his prior promise to himself. The decision is now out of his hands: the die is cast. His self-imposed discipline—his responsibility to his prior decision—forces him to become irresponsible and untrustworthy, to leave his familiar, authentic, comfortable, prudent self, to emerge beside himself. Knowing himself freed *and buoyed by the knowledge that he can bear it*, he is—the word is precise —ecstatic.

Mechanisms for breaking old routines are of course well known. To become deranged we schedule carnivals, masquerades, and saturnalia. We buy extended season's tickets to disorienting performances. We talk ourselves into previously unplayed roles with such *deliberate* recklessness that we finally feel forced to honor our pretensions. We pledge ourselves to a college education, knowing we will have to play a part in unfamiliar courses in which we are quite literally tested. We decide on new careers and trial marriages (though we still decline to make irreversible contracts to ensure recurrent separations and new ventures). Such contracts establish new situations which

---

Not to make men "better," not to preach morality to them in any form, as if "morality in itself" or any ideal kind of men were given; but to create conditions *that* require stronger men *who for their part need, and consequently will have, a morality (more clearly: a physical-spiritual discipline)* that makes them strong.

—Friedrich Nietzsche

---

in turn induce us to change our conduct. We enter them because we know how futile it is to try to change oneself directly by a sheer act of will. We can't break a habit or get ourselves to relax by simply willing it. I may will something, but the "I" which makes this decision has no force of its own, and our will needs a lever. Although we may know it would be "good" for us to jump into the water, we can't make ourselves do it—not until we have first moved into a line that permits no escape at the critical moment. That is, by committing ourselves to people who differ from us, whom we envy for taking chances while we are merely prudent, we find ourselves caught in motion and having new experiences.

And those individuals whose work has the effect of helping us move in ever-widening circles we esteem as models. Whether educators, psychiatrists, parents, or artists, we appreciate them as agents of change—not, clearly, because they tell us *what* to do but because they take the lead in removing impediments to action. They unmask, desublimate, and demystify. Opening stages for action, they free us to reveal our own unrealized potentials.

Yet before rushing ahead to capture ground on which to develop our capacities, it is best to consider the cost of alarming and abusing those who happen to have found a home, settled in, and armed themselves. I would pause before asking them to risk *their* hard-won achievement—the peace they have succeeded in making with themselves. Because they *like* it where they are, our activities may impel them not to question themselves but to attack us. It is best therefore to start with ourselves where we are and take but small steps. Merely bearing witness, we will then perhaps attract distraught neighbors without arrogantly insinuating how generously we are spending our lives for them. Thus we might note publicly that we have come to the end of

---

Does all this mean a surrender to the silence of those European philosophers and to the melancholy of those European revolutionaries who let history end with America and prophesy a nihilism that will reveal itself as fascism? By no means: there is no reason for European history to repeat itself on American ground after America has reached its end. The demythifying of America is not the end of America but rather the end of a specific consciousness.

—Manfred Henningsen

---

an era, that we desire a future unburdened by any authentic meaning, that ours is a moving present, an opportunity for living beyond hope and for sharing the distinctive qualities of our hopelessness. We can proceed to pry open what are currently our own most precious possessions—our own circumscribed selves, our family, home, school, job, and country. We can enclose each of these entities in quotation marks so as to indicate that we only *call* them that and are ready to suit more of ourselves by calling them something else.

8

Theaters of Operation

It scarcely matters what the action is, whether it is growing food, taking a walk, building a house, telling a story, preparing a meal, or making love. You can treat all activities as if they were ongoing processes meant to come to no end, meant to give you nothing but the pleasure of seeing yourself in action.

Starting is hardest. How can you start building a house if you don't know *what* you're starting? How can you go anywhere if you don't know your destination? How begin if you don't know the end? How do the right thing if you don't know what it's right *for*?

There are ways.

Treat time as yours and clear some space. Take a deep breath and then start doing it, right or wrong. Make a minimal gesture, perhaps merely proclaiming aloud, "I don't seem to be able to do anything"—and thereby find yourself doing something, the proclamation itself denying your despair.

Having made time and space, draw a boundary, sketch in some background, select and place your props, and start the music with a nod to the drums. Make a scene of sorts, a setting capable of holding action—but nothing overpowering. At the same time (yes, you need to be everywhere at once) move in your characters, a cast with distinctive temperaments and dispositions. If your characters seem listless and wooden, give them details, charms, quirks, complications. Bestow further dimensions, greater promises. And keep prodding your background so that it will not relax and recede. Now (if not before) signal your audience. Let it enter, just as I am letting you know by my disconnected prose that you, too, may get involved and fill things in. Keep orchestrating scenery, sounds, actors, and audience. Encourage whatever elements are weakest, confiding in them that they can be trusted. Make it apparent that you are confident that they will be all right on their own, that by participating they will create their own coherent selves.

Trust them and your material. Don't polish, censor, or judge. Enlarge the action so that banalities will fall of their own weight. Keep moving. Don't follow some theory of acting, some manual for growing food, taking a walk, building a house, telling a story, preparing a meal, or making love. Go with the action—cajoling, enticing, facilitating, mediating, applauding.

And whenever you get a glimpse of yourself, allow yourself to *like* the way you're doing it, the way you're letting it happen, the way you give life to a world of waiting props, characters, audiences—your very self—in space you cleared, time you made.

The only promising spaces for practical action as I have indicated are those in which we currently find ourselves—our apartments and suburbs, offices and workshops, educational and recreational institutions. We are less in need of lofty plans for transforming closed institutions into ongoing processes than of making specific moves where, as it happens, we have the power to act. To develop our potentialities and augment our lives, we must proceed concretely to demystify and redefine the existing structures of our marriages and families, our educational and professional activities.

We are initially handicapped in making these moves by conventional notions of how our lives ought to be organized and governed. Our organizations make little sense to us unless they are directed to fulfill some predetermined goal. Thus our expectations of Private Life or Professional Obligation make it hard to develop new aspects of ourselves. As we bring the array of our various activities to what we assume to be their *proper* end, we feel it is only natural to repress our natural urges.

Sexual practices—I would wish to start close to home—reveal how ingeniously the liberal concern with achieving end results remains constant despite changing expectations. Although the organization of sex, the very stage for it, has assuredly been enriched during recent decades, the belief persists that sexual activities must have some extrinsic point. The problem therefore continues to be one of technique. The basic rule is clear: success in sex depends on novelty, role reversals, violations of accepted conventions. Only by contradicting prevailing expectations can we arouse interest or generate rage, cause the pulse to beat faster and the blood to well up. Today, conventional life is felt to be cold and competitive. Instructed to reverse this experience by the latest liberal sex manual, we reject coldness and competitiveness, abusive language and rough gestures: they cannot serve to arouse because they are familiar. Since only unfamiliar experiences excite us, we must now conduct ourselves as soft and responsive, as submissive underachievers, our manner forbearing, voice gentle, language unpolished. The times demand that we use a strategy of not trying so that, duly touched, we will make it.

Thus by resolute disarming, our latest power play is staged. Openness and spontaneity become modish instruments—new sublimations conforming to a myth that directs us to keep means separate from ends, to keep calculating advantages. Remaining manipulative, we use "play" and "openness" to

Consider someone moving within your range who seems to be quite indifferent to being witnessed. He seems to squander whatever talent he may have for self-assertion, indolently going his way—not insisting on doing so, merely doing it. He is complacent, at most bemused by the competitive games of his contemporaries. You may find it hardly credible that he does not deliberately seek to display himself as playing the role of someone unconcerned about the impression he might make. Is he really indifferent about leaving his mark—some imprint at least of modesty? Or does he actually want you to take note of his undemanding posture because he suspects that your noting it may yet turn out to be to his advantage?

Perhaps his lassitude actually comes naturally to him: he does not have the stomach for competing or success has turned him sour. Perhaps he really doesn't much care to assert himself and is beyond the reach of those who remark he will never have anything to show for his existence. You wonder if possibly he just doesn't care to show that he is unconcerned about achieving anything memorable.

Beginning to recognize him, you wonder how you might suit him, how you might accommodate that part of yourself which he embodies so fully. Now that you see him—the nonchalant, careless part of yourself—you think of making room for him. But how? How would you reconstruct society, all the prevailing ways of surviving, all the conventional ways of feeling pleased? How would you change yourself?

score. Committed to whatever practice is the latest idealized enticement—to the transgression of normalcy currently known as "mellowness"—we are but new technicians working in behalf of reified sex. To touch and relate, our means—not our ends—are sincere language, sentimental gestures, unobtrusive measures. Our instruments are whatever fantasy or routine might go against the current grain, whatever moves us efficiently toward success.

When we treat some kinds of conduct as efficient and others as wasteful we necessarily have some objective in mind and become preoccupied with how to realize it. The cost of having predefined objectives, as I have so far merely implied, is limited participation: as we grant life to prevalidated, abstracted, idealized parts of ourselves, we deny it to those parts which might yet be stimulated and come into play. Organizing libido in accordance with idealized abstractions, we become detached from what is "dirty" or "painful," from the displaced order of our unfelt excitements.

To the extent that we can desublimate—deprive endings of status—our latent political potentialities will be aroused. *By continuously bringing conflicting aspects of ourselves into a state of relation, we can eroticize— enliven—progressively more of our own existence.* We thereby engage in the march against the tyranny of genital over other aspects of sexuality. And as we begin to recognize unfamiliar parts of the body politic, we will also note how familiar and expressive organs still preside over a plurality of others. We will see in what ways tough, rigid, articulate leaders manage the diverse sensibilities of the rank and file, how those at the top maintain harmony among the mass of subordinate interests. They are representative organs speaking and gesturing for the mass of invisible others—others expected to remain untouched and lifeless within subordinate places.

I am making these observations not to idealize some existence free from structure and masculinity but rather to allow room for a postliberal discipline, an equalitarian order that would deny *any* specific interest a claim to preeminence, whether it be male or female, mind or body. To question the liberal notion that some discrete entity—currently a phallic one—properly can represent all others is to undermine incumbents who are secure and erect in office. Demythifying the armory of liberal defense mechanisms will arouse underprivileged parts of the body politic and open the way to their fuller participation. Ideally, new interests will emerge and play on terms of equality in shared spaces and shared times—not, I should add, *proper* spaces or *good* times (not their opposites either), merely shared ones, no others remaining after the Myth of Liberalism has been deflated and the reified organs of the state have withered away.

Just as demythifying sex roles opens the way to increased participation, so do efforts to break down stereotyped conceptions of The Married Couple or The Family. Once aware of the routinized intimacy of what has become idealized as Marriage, we can begin to envisage promising alternatives—at the same time guarding against being so carried away by some idealized vision of open marriage that it, too, emerges as but another fixation. We should be able to see the opportunities offered by a domestic stage on which people meet to confirm their differences and thereby give life to previously undisclosed aspects of themselves. On such a stage (a model for other stages) adults work to provide for themselves and ultimately for whomever they can include to give more color and variety to their existence—friends and children who are bound to test their capacity for breaking old patterns and displaying new ones.

Such a household includes not only its children but also the sick and the old. Not transfixed by the invisible walls built around The Family, the two people who are its natural nucleus grow by including unfamiliar outsiders and new projects. Moreover, they support one another as they seek to identify new parts of themselves independent of their relationship, whether in solitude or with outsiders. In their independence, they remain dependent on a secure setting—call it "marriage"—in which to go on integrating their new experiences. Especially as they age and as their craving for growth through novelty wanes, they implicitly count on their retreat for sorting out and sharing their latest ventures, and for rehearsing new ones. Their home is sheltered space for mutual encouragement, space *reserved* for them, a place of trust that excludes only whoever threatens to keep them from sharing their experiences. Traveling lightly, we tend to forget the benefits of a durable center where we catch our breath and feel no need to repeat to each new partner in business or sex just how things have been with us before. We need someone who will listen to the latest escapade while still remembering the previous one, someone whose mere awareness of the past adds resonance to the present, someone at the heart of our lives where much goes simply without saying. Memory adds dimensions lost to those who merely travel.

My point is that we need familiar ground on which to *keep* relating—a common touchstone to measure our growth by. In the end, it is true, we may

---

Waste, decay, elimination need not be condemned: they are neces-sary consequences of life, of the growth of life. The phenomenon of decadence is as necessary as any increase and advance of life: one is in no position to abolish it. Reason demands, on the contrary, that we do justice to it.

It is a disgrace for all socialist systematizers that they suppose there could be circumstances—social combinations—in which vice, disease, prostitution, distress would no longer grow. But that means condemning life. A society is not free to remain young. And even at the height of its strength it has to form refuse and waste materials. The more energetical-ly and boldly it advances, the richer it will be in failures and deformities, the closer to decline. Age is not abolished by means of institutions. Neither is disease. Nor vice.

—Friedrich Nietzsche

---

all learn what we might not admit at the beginning—that our growth has been to no purpose. But this will not make us despair when we can continuously share experiences with others who remain present, who are as committed to encourage our departures as to welcome us back home.

Not only marriage and family, of course, but all other social arrangements for doing one's everyday work open possibilities for enlarged participation when they are accepted not as frozen ideals but as processes we ourselves put into motion. It is probably easiest to appreciate this kind of possibility in university settings. Scholars and scientists, teachers and students can be seen as a miniature social universe so organized that it will display in intensified form the full spectrum of interests which remain underdeveloped outside the university's gates. Serving no partisan interest, this community includes the old and the young, the infirm and the well; it accommodates vocational endeavors as diverse as medicine, law, sports, art, and commerce; it experiments with paramedicine, quasi-law, pseudosports, nonart, and nonprofit commerce.

The possibilities for enlarging educational settings of diverse interests are dramatically shown in what has become the most legendary of experimental colleges—Black Mountain College of North Carolina. Between its founding in 1933 and its demise in 1956, it was a dynamic, amorphous community, one given its full due in an account that itself demonstrates how the most conflicting of interests can be integrated between the covers of a book—Martin Duberman's *Black Mountain* (1972).

> A central aim was to keep the community small enough so that members could constantly interact in a wide variety of settings—not only at meals, but on walks, in classes, at community meetings, work programs, dances, performances, whatever. Individual life styles, in all their peculiar detail, could thereby be observed, challenged, imitated, rejected—which is, after all, how most learning proceeds, rather than through formal academic instruction. "You're seeing people under all circumstances daily," as Rice put it, "and after a while you get to the point where you don't mind being seen yourself, and that's a fine moment."
>
> All aspects of community life were thought to have a bearing on an individual's education—that is, his growth, his becoming aware of who he was and wanted to be. The usual distinctions between curricular and extracurricular activities, between work done in a classroom and work done outside it, were broken down.[1]

Not only did faculty and students and administrators—all of them teaching, all of them learning—freely drift in and out of the college but they also revealed how they could thrive by combining amateurism and professionalism, ineptness and talent, how they could make things happen—as in what was probably the first of those multimedia events that were called "happenings" in the 1960s. John Cage, as one participant recalls it, mounted a stepladder and "talked on the relation of music to Zen Buddhism, while a movie was shown, dogs barked, Merce Cunningham danced, a prepared piano was played, whistles blew, babies screamed, coffee was served by four boys dressed in white . . . and Edith Piaf records were played double-speed on a turn-of-the-century machine." As if impelled to demonstrate the promise of a postliberal world, all who were present found themselves free to follow their own impulses and yet to accept an underlying structure that coordinated their anarchy—a structure inducing self-awareness by emphasizing, as Duberman put it, "honesty in human interaction, distaste for an ethic of possession and accumulation, and the reserving of highest respect not for abstract intellect, but for how it showed itself, was used and was useful, in one's life."[2]

Black Mountain College intimates the possibilities for losing oneself in one's activities and thereby discovering organizing images on one's own. If current educational practices stress structures and disciplines which are *given*, we can redress the balance and cultivate practices that enable us to identify *with* phenomena, to affirm the world in *its* fullness and devote ourselves to *it*. Oriented by the pedagogy of John Dewey and Herbert Read, we can reinforce educational settings that encourage our innate capacity for using our own unconscious, prerational images to integrate our experiences. When

---

Gunnar Schonbeck, teacher, instrument maker and all-around music maker, inaugurated the Greenwall Music Workshop in the new Arts Center at Bennington College with an extravaganza, on March 17 that involved nearly 1,000 people in seven bands, four choruses, with faculty and student ensembles of the Music Division of the College.

The concert was the World Premiere of Schonbeck's "Collage No. 10," a two-hour piece involving, among other things, a revival of the Bennington College bell ringers (part of every commencement from 1936 to about 1953); speaking and-or singing solos by the acting president, Joseph S. Iseman, the chairman of the Board, Merrell Hambleton, the Dean of Faculty, Reinhoud van der Linde and Dean of Studies, Ronald Lee Cohen. They were accompanied by 40 chimes, some as long as 20 feet, some as short as three inches, 20 steel harps, 60 giant marimbas, seven bands, and an opera based on Bela Bartok's concept of a Serbo-Croatian Heroic Song.

The audience was asked to sing, hum, make sounds and noises, and otherwise participate in "Collage No. 10." Schonbeck positioned the various bands, choruses, instruments and participants around the mammoth music workshop and pieced their music together in a kind of Ivesian sound collage.

Also participating were the 150-member Hoosick Falls Senior Band, the 75-member Hoosick Falls Junior Band, the 100-member Cambridge Senior Band, the Mount Greylock Symphonic Winds (90 members), the North Bennington Junior Band (40 children), the 150-voice Cambridge Central Chorus, and the 150-voice Hoosick Falls Central Chorus. Along with a 10-member Bennington College faculty ensemble, a 100-student orchestra, and some 50 guest artists.

"Collage No. 10" comes in three parts, each about the same length. The first part is called commencement, and is based on the traditional Bennington College version of it. Bell ringers rerang the virtually forgotten college alma mater song, "Bright Sing nor Sigh," written the second semester by a student in 1933. Chimes were played and various people spoke as part of the beginning celebration of the new Arts Center.

The second part is the opera. It is based on the Serbo-Croatian Heroic Song entitled "The Captivity of Dulic Ibrahim." The narrator was drama instructor Leroy Logan, and Richard Frisch, baritone, and Barbara Stein Mallow, cellist, performed solos. Several of the choruses and Bennington faculty and student musicians also participated.

The finale involved every participant and member of the audience. Each band and chorus had five minutes in which to play whatever it

wanted, and Schonbeck pulled it all together in his aural collage. The
audience hummed, the marimbas, steel harps, steel drums and a hammer
dulcimer ensemble accompanied while Gunnar Schonbeck whirled in the
midst of it all, like an itinerant alchemist pulling the sounds out of
anything and everyone present.

—Bennington College *Quadrille*, Spring 1976

these images are not developed because they are not allowed free expression,
our knowledge of ourselves, one another, and our environment is constrained.
We both know and experience less when we are trained to conform to
predefined, pretested structures, embracing established forms of rationality,
patterns that are *given* us—as when we are told about things we have not
experienced. What is then deadened is our own *natural* capacity for ordering
our feelings and composing ourselves. This deadening occurs, of course,
when dreaming, fantasizing, and playing are relegated to the margin of the
curriculum, treated as "mere" art and discredited as "only" subjective.
Unwelcomed, our imagined realities are then kept from developing in their
full sensuousness. Our stories, like our relationships, become prosaic and
dull. We lose our power to imagine and empathize and relate.

Although Black Mountain College and the uncounted experimental
colleges which flourished in the 1960s are defunct, it surely remains possible
to add commonly disregarded concerns to existing educational settings. Even
when such efforts fail to achieve their explicit objectives they can serve to
reactivate those who engage in them. A sequence of memoranda that moved
back and forth within my own university department shows on the most
pedestrian level how new issues surface when a community—a mere Department of Political Science—considers making its life more dynamic and
various by including interests relegated to the margin. At the time I urged in
an open memorandum that a departmental student-faculty relations committee
accept a greater degree of equality. A colleague, Professor Rudolph Rummel, addressed a public memorandum to the same committee. There were
further waves—as shown in part by the succession of memoranda that appear
on the following pages.

The dimensions of feasible action are hardly disclosed by exchanges of
academic memoranda. Far greater and also more revealing possibilities for
enlarging communities are provided by Joshua Horn's account of the organization of medicine in contemporary China. An English surgeon practicing in
China in the 1950s and 1960s, he was involved in a social enterprise of such
massive scale that its ramifications appear in sharp relief. Horn's *Away with
All Pests* (1969) dramatizes the inevitable conflict between widespread

UNIVERSITY OF HAWAII

Department of Political Science

MEMORANDUM   September 1, 1968

TO: Yas Kuroda, Chairman
       Student-Faculty Relations Committee

FROM: Henry Kariel

I feel our committee has the chance to do something of significance
for the Department and (who knows?) the rest of the University.

We ought to regard the Department as including all undergraduate majors,
graduate students, teaching assistants, research assistants, faculty
members, and administrative personnel. I would assume that, although
the interests of these groups conflict, we are nonetheless engaged
in a common enterprise. Moreover, I would assume that all individuals
affected by the policies adopted for the pursuit of our shared objectives
should have an equal opportunity to participate in formulating policy.
Accordingly, I would urge that all legislative power be placed in the
Department -- inclusively defined. Probably, the Department will wish
to delegate some of its powers to a representative executive committee
as well as to committees concerned with implementing general policies.
The Department will in any event have the authority to adopt its rules
of procedure, to elect its officers, and to establish committees concerned
with such matters as recruiting, admissions, promotions, curriculum,
external relations, etc.

Why proceed along the lines I have sketched out? Partially for
prudential reasons, in anticipation of student pressure. Partially
because it will help us identify latent, unexpressed interests.
Partially because it will add life to departmental affairs. And
partially because we might publicly demonstrate the uses of democracy.

It may be objected that we would have to pay an exorbitant price for
pursuing some of our present projects democratically; I would hope,
however, that the Department -- again, inclusively defined -- could
be persuaded of this and authorize such projects to operate under
nondemocratic norms (just as we rarely allow for democracy in military
establishments or mental hospitals). It may be objected that few
individuals are really so interested in politics that they would
wish to participate in departmental decision making; but I would not
find such indifference objectionable as long as the opportunity for participation is genuine. It may also be objected that the University
administration would never tolerate genuine democracy; in response, I
would only suggest we treat this proposal as an experimental design
and proceed to test what is alleged to be reality.

September 9, 1968

MEMORANDUM

To: Yas Kuroda, Chairman, Student-Faculty Relations Committee and All
        Department Members

FROM: Rudy Rummel

RE: An Open Memorandum to the Kuroda Committee from Henry Kariel

        Henry argues for enveloping the department in a democratic cloak,
whose folds would include faculty, students, and administrative personnel. (I
gather janitresses are excluded by not being exclusively on Department payroll.
Why should this be so? Since janitresses service our Department, they should,
according to his credo, be included in the community. Then, why not the
campus mailman, switchboard operator, and security men? Surely all the
Deans and sundry administrative personnel should be included. Now,
somewhere along the line shouldn't all students be included also?
Then, we would have satisfied the ideal: a truly democratic Department
within which tenure, hiring, curriculum and grades are decided by representatives elected to the Department and whose chairman is elected by the
University as a whole. Anything less must compromise Henry's ideology.)
His argument consists of five assertions: democratization would

   (1) anticipate student pressure,

   (2) help identify latent, unexpressed interests,

   (3) add life to Department affairs,

   (4) publicly demonstrate uses of democracy,

   (5) make us more professional about our pretensions and less preten-
        tious about our profession.

        To paraphrase and consolidate Henry's view, our professional policies
should help spread his ideology. For his position reduces to importing

into our professional concerns the political ideology giving him most comfort.

Were an ideology to dominate by virtue of its norms and not its functions, consider the consequences -- consequences that may have already been manifest in some department affairs. Major criteria for evaluating prospective faculty would rest on their sympathy for these norms -- those unsympathetic (by being "pro-establishment" or having worked in the CIA or DOD?) would not be kindly considered.

Perhaps most subversive of our professional goals in the long run, would be the conflict generated within an ideologized Department. No two people view the same ideology alike. Ideological schools equally perceiving themselves as sealed in democratic plastic will contend; the Department will become a political arena in which questions of merit, tenure, hiring, courses, committee memberships, salary, and student participations are filtered through factional political conflict.

If we are not to ideologize the Department, then on what are our decisions to be based? The answer is so simple and, I would have once assumed, so much a part of our profession that I hesitate to express it. Our decision framework should help us achieve our professional goals: contributing to knowledge, educating the interested in our accumulated knowledge and enabling them to expand that knowledge. These are the criteria for our choice between alternatives, including student participation in the Department. For, to borrow David Tabb's words, these would "make us more professional about our pretensions and less pretentious about our professions."

TO   Rudy et al.

FROM: Henry S. Kariel

SUBJECT: Democratizing the Department (Still)

Rudy is right: I am not opposed to a charter. I believe in
law and order. But I also think that the authority for a charter is
properly derived from the consent of those governed by it. There are
crisis situations (the life of a community itself may be at stake)
when one cannot afford to operate on the basis of such consent. But
our survival is hardly in question; surely we still have time to
persuade one another of the desirability of accepting one or another
charter; surely (I would argue) we need not substitute power for
reason. In short, I would think we can risk enlarging our Department
along the lines I sketched out in my initial memo -- and we might
then adopt an acceptable committee structure.

I should add that, unlike Rudy, I do not think of democratic
norms as ideology, that is, as false consciousness. I do think it
can be shown that the various arguments for rejecting democratic
norms are all ideological: they serve some special interest -- though
not necessarily the CIA's, the DoD's, or Rudy's.

Finally, I wonder how the professional goals enumerated by Rudy --
goals I share -- can be realized without a commitment to democratic
procedures. Doesn't it remain to be demonstrated empirically that
meritocracies (except under crisis condition) are the proper model
for educational institutions?

MEMORANDUM   September 30, 1968

TO: Political Science Faculty

FROM: Rudy Rummel

RE: Ideologizing the Department and Henry Kariel's Latest Memo.

Can educational institutions be anything other than meritocracies?
If not on merit, how do we decide among students requesting admission?
If not on merit, how do we grade our students? If not on merit, how
do we grant degrees to some students (and deprive others)? If not
on merit, how do we select our colleagues? If not on merit, how do
we renew contracts, grant tenure, give merit raises, and salary
adjustments? Or are we to admit all applicants to our "community"
and automatically grant degrees, renew contracts, confer tenure?

Oh yes, may come the responses, but democratic procedures can
be employed to define and apply merit criteria. Will these procedures be democratic, however, or themselves based on merit?
Here is the point of friction some may ignore, but which succeeds
in wearing down democratic pretensions to meritocratic bedrock.

How are democratic votes in our department to be allocated?
(It is the right to vote on competing alternatives that is the
discriminating characteristic of democratic procedures, and not the
right to participate. Some totalitarian societies are noted for their
mass participation, as are mobs, gangs, and lynching parties.)
Should each student, secretary, and faculty member be given one vote in
the beginning to select their teachers for the year? Or must they
select teachers from an approved pool, say of those with certain
degrees (and in a certain area or field?)? However, merit then becomes
a necessary condition for selection.

Enough! One doesn't have to wash a whole window to see through
it. Or do I have the wrong window? Can one really have democratic
Department procedures that are not basically meritocratic? Let's
see your charter, Henry.

participation in defining the goals of medical practice and decision-making by professionals. His uncritical Maoism may lead him to exaggerate, but it does give a clear view of China's community of physicians, nurses, aides, administrators, party functionaries, patients, and relatives—all interacting in a equalitarian manner. It is manifestly a community for which health care is not an end product but an ongoing process. Its members are devoted to the task of reducing suffering, but far more basically to continuously redefining what constitutes "suffering"—or its opposite, "well-being." They do not assume that the doctor alone knows best what is really meant by illness or health. They are so organized that *all* affected interests participate in identifying their discomforts—including the subtle, incalculable discomfort that people experience when they are stereotyped and treated as *mere* medical subordinates, *mere* careerist physicians, *mere* clinical cases, *mere* administrators, or, worst of all, *mere* patients who are but objects to others.

Horn knows, of course, that if every member of the medical community were forever taking turns to play every conceivable part, the benefits due to specialization would be lost. What chance would there be to make medical discoveries in the absence of professional training, long-range planning, fragmented labor, and dedication to a singular objective? What care could then be given to the marginal case? Could uncommon illness be treated as efficiently? Yet, however great the benefits of goal-oriented hierarchic organization, the Chinese experience does expose at least one incalculable price that is invariably paid for them: the individual's alienation from others and from his work. Though it is hard to calculate the malaise and pain and disease that result from alienation, they are nonetheless the costs of nonparticipation, inequality, and hierarchy. What is gained by demystifying an abstract, elite-defined concept of "illness" and "health" is the participation—the nonalienation—of everyone affected by medical treatment. Doctors, nurses, orderlies, pharmacists, patients, and yes, janitors enter the profession. They discuss common problems, criticizing one another, and see their work from the point of view of others. Administrators, Horn notes, do manual work, "sweeping the floors, stoking the furnaces or serving food. . . . When a hospital director cleans a ward, he does so under the direction of the ward orderly who can form a first-hand estimate of his attitude and deflate any tendency toward superiority."[3] Nurses become doctors while patients become diagnosticians. The arrogant are reduced to listeners while the humble gain in self-esteem and speak up. Untrained peasant doctors become general practitioners. Although specialized roles remain, those who play them keep rotating—and slowly redefine them. The boundaries go, the center will not hold, and people move in permanent revolution.

I realize I have let the final part of this picture turn into *my* fantasy. Nevertheless, fantasies dramatize the pathos of real situations. Even Horn's account, less of a hyperbole than my summary, can serve to expose what it costs to keep politics *out* of medical practice. Thus Horn has made a reviewer of his book, James Gordon, sensitive to the American alternative:

> Our hospitals are run from the top down. Doctors write "orders" for treatment; nurses and their aides carry them out. Hospital administrators coordinate the activities of the various clinical services and oversee their financing. Ward clerks, kitchen help, maids, janitors, orderlies, and lab technicians, unacquainted with the patients, do the menial work. Patients, often bewildered about the diagnosis, submit to treatment. Criticism generally is directed by a higher status person to a lower—a senior physician to a resident, a resident or a nursing supervisor to a nurse. Physicians get together for conferences in which free play of ideas is encouraged, but the discussion is almost always related to a specific and specifically medical problem; only occasionally are nurses present. No one would think to invite a ward clerk or maid; and patients, except when present to illustrate "an interesting clinical finding," are strictly forbidden.[4]

The hierarchical organization of medicine follows ineluctably from the belief that medical practice has an unambiguous objective: the individual patient's health. When this is presumed to be the indubitable ideal for the entire society, it becomes only reasonable to frustrate the participation of subordinates in the hierarchy and of such "outsiders" as nurses, administrators, patients, relatives, and the infinite number of potential patients. Their involvement is not *regarded* as healthy. It cannot be seen to constitute an enlargement of well-being, of that satisfaction which is a byproduct of one's contribution to a common enterprise.

How far it is feasible to promote political development and strengthen communal as opposed to individualistic tendencies even within settings that are partially goal-oriented is illustrated in Bruno Bettelheim's reports on his work with autistic and schizophrenic children at the University of Chicago's Orthogenic School. To the extent that infantile autism is an extreme manifestation of the individualism of the liberal society, Bettelheim's project can provide clues for moving beyond liberalism. As he describes autism in *The Empty Fortress* (1967) and *A Home for the Heart* (1974), it is the condition of children who are wholly bewildered, given to either total withdrawal or mindless violence. They fail altogether to relate. To see and define and accept themselves—and then to establish connections with others—the Orthogenic School seeks to enable them to unlearn what they have been trained to accept: an everyday discipline which killed their natural inclination to express themselves, to play, symbolize, and talk.

Bettelheim's work clarifies what kind of institutional support is required for personality development, what kind of elaborate structure is needed to encourage children to act. He shows how imperative it is for the staff to accept their every outburst and respond affirmatively to their most attenuated efforts to communicate, their most private of languages. The administrative structure must be such as to deflect every effort to impose a predefined order on children; it must oppose all attempts to recondition them by the self-destructive technique of reinforcing approved behavior. What Bettelheim calls "milieu therapy" requires that patients find themselves in warm and open dormitories governed by rules which relate staff to patients rather than protect either group from experiencing the other.

Although Bettelheim's patients are extreme cases, his approach to healing has general relevance. However developed a community may deem itself, its members are always at least partially autistic—that is, arrested in their development, not wholly capable of grasping and integrating new experiences. Every society suffers from shocks and depressions aggravated by a separation of means from ends and by a division of labor which retards action

---

Rather than racing full speed ahead toward industrialization in the customary manner, with emphasis on modern technology, economic efficiency, bureaucratic control, and elitist decision-making, the Chinese are deliberately encouraging much use of "inefficient" industry, "non-expert" personnel, "irrational" allocation of resources, and "uninformed" decision-making. The result, at least in the short run, is a slower pace of growth in the most sophisticated sectors of the economy and society, but also a country where, for the sake of social justice and maximal development of human potentialities, everyone participates in learning, in developing skills, in governing, and in acquiring a sense of purpose and self-respect.

—Oliver Lee

---

and finally boxes us in altogether. To free autistic individuals and generate social development requires us to break boundaries by being infinitely receptive to unspoken intimations and to barely expressed needs. It demands accepting unseemly gestures and dirty words, being grateful for each of them, encouraging society to come to terms with infantile forms of behavior, with extremism and violence.

Bettelheim's methods for extending participation may well be thought of as a model not only for mental institutions but for all institutions whatever. The Orthogenic School reveals in concentrated form what is appropriate for all enclosures, the closed structures of society as well as the closed minds of professional personnel. *When excluded interests freely enter and imprisoned ones freely exit—that is, when participation in human enterprises is enlarged—the end of the enterprise and the means for achieving it become one and the same.* Participation is at once a means and an end. It carries its own reward —the immediately gratifying knowledge that one is in the process of expressing unrealized interests in some public arena, that one's own interests are being integrated with those advanced by others, that all are sharing in the construction of social reality. Recognizing this process as politics, we can see all medical practice—our life generally—being enriched precisely because it is politicized.

Our lives necessarily become impoverished when elite-formulated criteria of "rationality" organize human endeavors so as to limit participation. It is best, I think, to elaborate on this proposition by testing it in the field of medicine where it would seem most dubious. After all, who would not consider it "rational" to restrict participation so as to save lives? What constitutes life-saving would seem to be so far beyond question that it would appear only proper to allow experts to prolong life at all costs. Yet the way we have come to think about life and death—one *opposed* to the other, and each

---

Health and sickness are not essentially different, as the ancient physicians and some practitioners even today suppose. One must not make of them distinct principles or entities that fight over the living organism and turn it into their arena. That is silly nonsense and chatter that is no good any longer. In fact, there are only differences in degree between these two kinds of existence: the exaggeration, the disproportion, the nonharmony of the normal phenomena constitute the pathological state. . . .

—Friedrich Nietzsche

---

neatly circumscribed—has consequences which raise doubts about our conclusions. We regard both life and death as wholly the individual's property. One's life belongs to the individual no less than one's death. He is free within the limits of his economic resources to do with himself as he sees fit. It is deemed to be one of the glories of liberalism that he may extend his life as long as his cash holds out. His existence is not assumed to be rooted in the sphere of politics, in what a larger public might define as reasonable, in a shared rationality.

And the experts he pays to maintain *his* life and forestall *his* death—nurses, pharmacists, administrators, physical therapists, physicians, lab technicians, psychiatrists—understandably have the same view. Trained to fight death, the doctor is alienated from experiences associated with it, whether they are located within himself or find expression in the old and the dying. For him, death as process inexorably connected with life, death as ever-present part of living, has simply no *professional* standing. He feels no need to support something as vague as man-living-and-dying-in-society. Instead he is prepared to oppose Death—a fixed, reified, autonomous abstraction. He feels no need to inquire whether the community, in order to flourish, requires the death of what we treat as individual organisms. The focus is on giving birth, saving life, and prolonging it—indeed, on "keeping alive." For the physician as professional, dying is an unambiguous disaster. Nothing in the Myth of Liberalism can validate his support of the *process* of dying. He fights Death, and when Death wins, he feels he loses.

Questioning this doctrine, Talcott Parsons has recently argued for incorporating other than narrow medical interests in medical practice. He has noted that once the individual's life—death's reified opposite—ceases to be treated as the singular end of man's shared existence, the physician and everyone else involved in healing can see living and dying ecologically in relation to social needs. It then becomes possible to assume responsibility for more diverse aspects of human nature, including *whatever* aspects enrich it, dying not excluded.

Such an expanded ethic makes us sensitive to conditions under which our conventional idealizing of individual life violates our social nature. The price paid for an individual life can turn out to be the misery of the patient and his family. And given the human and natural energies used for the maximum-intensity care of individuals, the price surely includes the depletion of natural resources in the service of a narrowly circumscribed interest. There is good reason, in short, for broadening the prevailing conception of the "rational" organization of medical practice:

> The relativized ethic provides a greatly enhanced basis for recognizing the consummatory meanings of death. The impending, inevitable death of a patient need not be taken as defeat of treatment. The efforts of the physician may then—in a certain sense—facilitate the patient's death, supporting his sense of dignity and his ability to put his affairs in order, encouraging a readjustment in his relations with his family, and meliorating the trying conditions of a death. These activities also aid the patient to employ his "gifts of life," but involve the mastery of death as social and psychological rather than physiological processes.

A relativized medical ethic, as Parsons calls it, allows us to question professionally specialized confrontations with death and respond to interests other than narrowly "life-saving" medical ones. Thus Parsons has cautiously urged that we make room for a greater variety of experts—"psychiatrists, social workers, ethicists, theologians, lawyers, and social scientists, among others."[5]

No doubt, involving such professionals in decision-making would extend the range of strictly medical expertise and constitute a move toward a postliberal society. To go further, however, life and death would have to be recognized as integrated in an ongoing organic process rather than as ontological polarities—one good, the other evil—the evil to be eradicated with every means at the disposal of a technological society. Such a shift in viewpoint would make it possible to approach the sick and the old not as alien elements but as members of the community. They would be treated not as unproductive resources that ought to be helped (as Americans say) to help

themselves so that they can "contribute to society" but as expressions of life
which remind everyone of estranged parts of himself.

To note how the notion of individual life has become a fixed end is to
jeopardize the organization of medicine just as the demystification of *any*
fixed end jeopardizes the professionalism required to attain it. And if
professionalism itself is in jeopardy, so are the agencies which maintain it—
admission boards and testing centers that certify an individual as competent
insofar as he possesses skills for implementing a given goal. Once we accept
that our interests are served when we keep goals from congealing, the
authority of all professionalism becomes suspect. When we treat knowledge
not as some stable body of facts but as unstable expression of ever-variable
shared experiences, as subject to continuous change because its formulation is
an ongoing social activity, experts lose their warrant to claim knowledge of
what it means to be properly schooled, properly married, properly employed,
or properly alive. They cannot claim to *know* what it means to live (or die)
properly. Knowledge of what it means to live well, it then becomes evident,
can come only from those who participate in the process of living, not from
authorities trained to "know best."

It may of course be argued that without judgments of competence based on
a professionally established body of knowledge, organizations cannot
function efficiently: inequality, it may be insisted, is the prerequisite for
productivity. In a joint study, Richard Sennett and Jonathan Cobb have
reflected precisely on this argument:

> Affluent societies have crossed a line beyond which that justification, were it
> ever true at all, no longer matters. The problem confronting an affluent capitalist
> society is not how to make more things, but how to get rid of what it has. The fact
> that the United States has arrived at a condition where so much more can be
> produced than is needed means this country can also afford to stop the divisive
> process of evaluation without threatening survival. We can now afford, if that is
> the term, to recognize a diversity, rather than a hierarchy of talents, that is, do
> away with shaming; it is no longer necessary, if it ever was, for organizations to
> make a few individuals into the "best" and treat the rest as an undifferentiated
> mass.[6]

In relatively secure social settings it becomes possible to give up our reified
virtues and cease deferring to those said to possess them. Making the very
notion of some abstract worthiness suspect by obliterating the distinctions
established by professionalism, we reduce what Sennett and Cobb have called
the hidden injuries of class. We rehabilitate the sense of personal worth of the
mass of people at the margin and bottom of industrial society.

One alternative course of action for enabling people to gain in self esteem
is no longer open to us. We cannot go back to the preliberal society which

assigned everyone a predetermined place. It is of course comforting to contemplate a society in which peasants were no more able to rise than aristocrats to fall. If servants performed menial labor or masters had to assume responsibility for the lower strata of society, neither could be resentful. After all, it was but their fated part in the nature of things. Moreover, every person had the support of others who shared his burden: a sense of community could make everyone's fate meaningful and bearable. It would surely be consoling to find oneself authoritatively placed.

Yet the faith in social hierarchy ordained by Nature has been so shaken as to be no longer available. The Liberal Enlightenment of the eighteenth century successfully undermined it by insisting on public equality—thus making room for a private sector in which man's unequal talents would be unequally rewarded. This private sector opened the whole of society to men (and ultimately to women) who could demonstrate competence and merit. Today, we are stuck with the consequences—entrenched professionals certifying that if you fail to move upwards, you must *deserve* to be where you are. If your place is lowly, you cannot blame society or those who have succeeded; you *alone* are responsible. You must make something of yourself by competing for scarce resources and investing your gains in the future or at least in your children. Yet as our future turns sour, as success makes us calloused, and as our children betray us, we wonder who is served by our drive for Ability, Talent, Quality, Merit, or Intelligence. Who profits when we conform to the approved definitions? And as it becomes clear how many diverse interests are repressed, it also becomes thinkable to withhold grades, credits, credentials, degrees, and certificates—and the privileges which accompany them. We learn to withhold judgment. Demystifying the notion of Ability, we see its significance in a larger social context, and we gradually recognize that its meaning is far from constant. The cameraman's ability to keep his subject steadily in focus is precisely the poet's disability. It all depends on our objective. But while the objectives we pursue do not define themselves, the mass of people scarcely have the opportunity to work out their own definitions. They are *led* to pursue what they are conditioned to identify as their own objectives. Only the few participate in deciding what the many are to live for. For most people, the ends are given. And those given ends determine, of course, what kind of behavior constitutes the ability to attain them. However, once we doubt the objective desirability of given ends and fixed roles, we wonder about the authority of those in power to call some kinds of behavior good and other kinds bad. It will all depend on what a man wants to be. It ceases to be defensible to judge Ability, Competence, Merit, and Quality in relation to a body of *objective* criteria. Yet such a collapse of standards need not leave us adrift in relativism. *We can still treat each of our acts as praiseworthy to the extent that they are manifestly incomplete—that is, open to further input, receptive to a greater degree of inclusiveness, ready to accommodate the results of future experience.* Thus our acts may be esteemed both for integrating the opposites into which we conventionally split the world and for displaying a lack of finality. No act of ours should impress anyone by virtue of its conclusiveness.

The demystification of objectified Ability and Expertise enables us to see that value lies in action when its objective is not some predefined end but the inclusion of whatever further experiences lie ahead. Moreover, it enables us

---

"Act your age!"

—American expression

---

to see that an education for inclusiveness requires an overcoming of the grading-and-degree system of pedagogy. As we learn to welcome every disruption of The Correct Way—every teacher's slap at certified coherence—we learn to certify our own way and our own coherence. We become self-confirming.

In the end, what we are left with as we learn to ignore established distinctions is an undefined potential—the possibility of a oneness which integrates prevailing polarities. We can acknowledge this oneness—this wholeness or integrity—whenever we happen to confront an act which embodies it, acknowledging the climber to be at one with the mountain, or the actor with the play.

But how can we tell whether or not their acts reflect such integrity? To measure them against some established standard would be once again to reify Ability. Yet if there is no pre-established, given standard, how can we tell whether a climber, writer, or actor will in fact, as the saying goes, have it together? Instead of looking for integrity, perhaps we would find it easier to look for signs of its absence. It is, after all, possible to tell that someone has not found his way when he *strains* to prove that he has. We can tell that he is at odds with himself, that he becomes angry at himself, that he tightens up and forces himself to eliminate those parts of his experience which he insists are "painful," that he does not treat himself and his world generously because, as he says, it would *hurt*. That is, we actually are not without knowledge of what is *all right*—namely a society in which we find ourselves stimulated and yet one without that strain we feel when we aim to reach an objective, to score, or to have something durable to show for our lives.

Such knowledge allows us to be discriminating and yet withhold credentials from anything that has been brought to completion. It justifies our confirming whatever act proclaims its own incompleteness, whatever form of conduct demonstrates the actor's ability to stay in rotation, to play at being a student and teacher, patient and doctor, prisoner and guard, loser and winner or to act—in Marx's romantic imagery—as shepherd, hunter, fisherman, and critic during different times of the day or night, never actually becoming so trapped in any of these roles as to resist moving on to another. What will justify our approval is not that a performance conforms to some abstract ideal but rather that it brings new experiences within the range of our attention, that it enables us to keep unfamiliar elements of life in suspense. Such a standard for judgment enables us to relax when we confront activities which get nowhere. We can accept them precisely because they do not move us closer to the truth—provided only they are ingenious enough to hold our interest. We can then appreciate activities because they are so structured as to keep us from arriving, because they encourage us to detour, elaborate, and digress, because they make us unconcerned about solving problems or effecting cures while leading us instead to extend our lives.

In the light of this standard, we can expect our activities to make us less narrow in our relationships because they *move* us. We will not be upset, for instance, if after psychoanalytic therapy the patient begins to discover nothing but a new order of discomforts. Nor will we disparage the medical profession because for every cured disease a new one appears. It will be good enough if the practitioner—*whoever engages in social action*—succeeds in elaborating on his existence. It will be sufficient if his interaction with others and his environment is so ingeniously intriguing that it brings aspects of his unlived life into being. .n this orientation, the practice of medicine—of healing—is laudable insofar as it enhances the life of the doctor. And if we refuse to settle who shall be doctor and who patient—if we deny that anyone *is* one or the other—there will be nothing selfish or elitist about this orientation. After all, we are committed to assume that it is in *everyone's* interest to change identities and roles, that fresh predicaments are always better than stale ones. Wanting to enrich the lives of doctors *and* patients, students *and* teachers, children *and* parents, we need only inquire how to provide facilities and occasions which allow individuals to help and heal and teach others—others who appear to be inert, blocked, or subnormal. Those who appear immature at the bottom must have chances for exchanging roles with those who appear mature at the top. Once we see maturity and immaturity as no more than appearances—as unreal acts—we can enlarge the stages for action. Once we cease to aim for real health or real knowledge, we can break out of that reified realm of being in which people simply *are*, in which doctors are bound to *be* doctors just as teachers are bound to *be* teachers. Once we have stopped aiming at true health and true knowledge we can realize that we are incurable, and that there is no more to life than the tone and style and resonance we ourselves are able to give it.

I would not want to insist on small beginnings and modest efforts before at least glancing at one larger possibility—the energy-releasing and community-extending effect of demystifying those grandiose objectives which are identified in the preamble of the United States Constitution—Union, Justice, Tranquility, Defense, and Welfare. Perhaps if their pervasive ambiguity—their inspired emptiness—were as obvious to Americans today as to The

Framers in 1789, there would be less eagerness to define the nation's Authentic Purpose. Americans might then recover the argument for expanding the sphere of the nation not because this will increase its power over others but because the citizenry would thereby become more colorful and its interests more various. The nation would cease to be regarded as a circumscribed arena with some singular temper. It would begin to release its trapped, bruised, and arrested inhabitants. And it would expose complexities apt to make it both harder and more exciting for its people to govern themselves.

To maintain a nation which would free human energies it seemed sufficient, at least at one time, to recognize the need to diversify individual interests by incorporating new regions and hence new economic pursuits. Today such efforts at diversification are frustrated by technology-induced standardization. The admission of Hawaii and Alaska to statehood, for example, may seem to have added flavor and color to America, yet in fact affected none of the underlying patterns of technologically controlled work and leisure. Nor is immigration apt to be significant: foreigners who seek admission have made prior adjustments to some stereotype of Americanism which all but cancels their eccentricities. What remains, then, as the alternative strategy for enlarging the size of the country is the clearing of specific, local space in which more private interests can become publicly visible.

In my concern for clearing space for staging new performances, I have moved toward increasingly larger institutional settings. Yet I would wish to keep returning to the beginning—not only to repeat that we can only commence with ourselves but also to add that I realize our stages for development are in fact meager. The lights are dim, and the possibilities for effective action may be near zero. Yet even at such times, I think we can still put pressure on our undivided selves and demystify the insidious notion that we must discover who we really are, acquire some true Individual Identity. It still remains possible, I think, to avoid shaping up, to operate a minimal theater of the divided self, a barely visible stage on which to leave small traces of doubt and duplicity. We can still make gestures that affect at least our own breath and pulse beat, that induce changes within ourselves. Parts of our mind and body can still resist, undulate, and make waves, providing minute evidence of exercises that transform a self alleged to be immutable, giving unsolicited testimony to our survival as actors dialectically in process while the world has chilled and night has become an oppressive giant.

To be sure, when sirens scream and mindless sadists furnish a murderous excess of excitement or when sheer banality terrorizes and *nothing* happens we may feel we have no choice but to remain stoically where we are. Even so, we can still show ourselves in the act of withdrawing, of not adding our weight to existing structures of power, not contributing to the harm being done to us. We can still express our resolve to keep waiting for things to happen. We can explicitly refuse to despair because we know that we can manage to live on almost nothing, that so far the future has always been different, that, although we *know* the present to be a horror, we have no conclusive evidence that the horror of the future (and of the *un*known past) must have the same texture. By assuming what is falsely thought to be a "merely" feminine posture—by waiting—we can still manifest our concern for new silences and spaces. We can make it easier for others who are equally near the end to watch us so that they too can learn to express themselves.

As we listen and wait, we will at least have done all we could to sustain the final peace which necessity reserves for us. We will have acted as if convinced that at least our primeval resoluteness will outlive us. One expert guide is Kafka. His strategy for coping when all exits are closed sustains the point which signifies our extinction: "So perhaps the best recourse is to meet everything passively, to make yourself an inert mass, and, if you feel that you are being carried away, not to let yourself be lured into taking a single unnecessary step, to stare at others with the eyes of an animal, to feel no compunction, in short, with your own hand to throttle down whatever ghostly life remains in you, that is, to enlarge the final peace of the graveyard and let nothing survive save that."[7]

Clearly, I am providing no positive idea of what it means to assume such an anticipatory posture. I can only note that there is no ready way to express an idea so negative and submissive, so lacking in that spirit of arrogant defiance stereotyped as masculine. There is no way to describe someone in the process of *expecting* the emergence of a new life. Nothing is manifest by which to distinguish between someone who has resigned from someone who

---

> He didn't fill his cup. "I'm not going," he said.
> "But you've got to do something."
> "Just not going."
> "Maybe you can say that's doing something."
> He drank part of his remaining coffee and looked up, not quite smiling. "It's not the same as not doing anything, is it?"

---

acts on his decision not to betray his expectancy because he knows the cost of betrayal. What unintrusive diagnostician can discern a withheld glow of anticipation or take note of someone's resolve to affirm an inclination he explicitly denies? What can I possibly say about someone who is forced to deny himself the visible reward of being seen in the process of refusing to despair? After all, he is doing nothing but awaiting a future community sufficiently alive to recognize his existence as having been one of invisible transactions, of mute refusals to surrender to the surface facts of experience.

At high noon, when nothing casts shadows and we cannot hide, we can still keep from trembling by recalling individuals whose transactions have impressed us as memorable and telling, who have found exemplary ways of dramatizing new human possibilities. Repeating legends or writing biographies, we can still act as their accrediting agents. As part of our own holding operation we can confirm the disruptive scenarios of such political actors as Thoreau or Malcolm X and make explicit how they extended an established balance of interests because they included outsiders who had previously subsisted at the margin. We can validate projects which transformed not only their authors but also some settled subject matter—whether the economy of Walden Pond or life in Harlem. Appreciating works by authors who have made themselves vulnerable, we can keep translating records of experience which, because they included both author and subject, have the power to move us, to make all of us accomplices in necessary crime.

I know of no better way of coming around to myself than to concede that I, too, seek to redeem my prose, appearing if not as author then at least as stage designer. There is good reason in any case for desublimating one's own projects (this essay included), for taking care to present no Data Bank of Useful Information, only oneself in the process of inviting readers to collaborate, to play (as I have tried) with no end in mind other than to get something out of one's own system, out of the works of others, out of whoever may listen. Bringing out is publishing, and I would want to publish both my ideas and the ideas of others as fully as I can. I would want to see how far I can go, not alone, but in public with others. Of course, as I lead readers (each representing some aspect of myself) into some sort of wilderness, I may so bewilder them that they fall by the way. Or I may lead them into territory so familiar to them that they will leave me and search for a more adventuresome guide. Yet my concern is always to stay doggedly in touch while moving. If my conceits or digressions cause others to act on their own and become authorities and authors, I can only hope they do as I do and invite me on *their* trips.

The writer's desire to finish is fatal to the truth. The End unifies. Unity must be established in another way.

—John Berger

In the meantime, I am buoyantly edging further away from reality, away from how things so manifestly are. Becoming ever less trustworthy, I work my way toward an unreal world where we are free to juxtapose our unaccredited lies to official truths, to give voice to whatever derangements we can invent, to attach new labels to all imaginable man-made occasions, to moments of irreducible madness.

9

Revolution

During revolutionary moments, stable regimes are unexpectedly demystified by the emergence of alternatives. Previously unheard outsiders rush into the public arena and make their mad, momentary appearance: workers, women, and students begin to speak out in public "possessed by a frenzied eloquence" (as Flaubert reported), improvising like children, dressing up for a new occasion, concerned with one another, and above all talking loosely, the words pouring out. During such radiant moments all conventional opposites would seem to merge—but not quite, for the participants still remain *aware* of one another's acts, of the new drama of their lives. They not only feel liberated from boredom but consciously celebrate their liberation. They are aware of the exalting spectacle—*calling* it a carnival, a festival, a masquerade—and are determined to recall and retell it. Theirs is no mere delirium but a *relating* of imagination and power, reality and magic, individual and society, art and life. The situations they create are utopian in the sense not that they achieve some final reconciliation of opposites but

---

Liberated from the constraints of time, place, circumstance, from history, men choose their parts from the available repertory or forge new ones in an act of creation. Dreams become possibilities. . . . Visibility, birth, entrance of human beings hitherto excluded from society. . . .

—Aristide R. Zolberg

---

rather that they constitute a world of sustained tension, each instant an achievement—what the surviving participants invariably report to have been an occasion for joy.

There should be no confusing such a moment with those which provide occasions for relaxing and letting go. The serenity it promises is that of the gyroscope, secure only when whirling. It is a state of tension beyond any specific good or evil. It allows a continuous testing of self, the kind of competition sustained by scientists and athletes and most fully revealed in the risks and strains of personal combat. William James knew that it was ignored by liberalism and called it war: "the supreme theater of human strenuous-ness." James (like Nietzsche) thought of it as a theater that needed to be kept open. To close it—or to treat it as a mere entertainment—was to leave people undeveloped in their capacity for seeing themselves and others under authentic pressure. Those who endure acting in it (Nietzsche was explicit on this point) see one another as a select company. They experience an *esprit de corps* contemptuous of any higher purposes, beyond loyalty to simple verities, beyond any ready-made patriotism.

Basically no other moments can justify our loyalty. No private time and space, no vacation or holiday away from them, no "time out" can be more precious. Ideally, they permeate the whole of our existence, making endings in our lives indistinguishable from beginnings. They take place in postliberal settings in which time itself is annihilated, in which the past is transcended: all caverns of love's body are touched and familiar, the mind has expanded, and there is no one who has not risen to fly with Yeats's falcon without falconer, "turning and turning in the widening gyre," gently whirling, easily switching from role to role. Men and women are in permanent revolution, bringing the world into museums and life into plays. At last, a world stage, a holy festival.

We have slowly become familiar with postliberal possibilities. The arts—all of them from sports to politics—keep providing us with prototypes, exemplary happenings such as diplomatic receptions, artist-designed earth-

---

> It is in the open air, under the sky, that you ought to gather and give yourselves to the sweet sentiment of your happiness. Let your pleasures . . . be free and generous like you are. . . .
>
> But what then will be the objects of these entertainments? What will be shown in them? Nothing, if you please. With liberty, wherever abundance reigns, well-being also reigns. Plant a stake crowned with flowers in the middle of a square; gather the people together there, and you will have a festival. Do better yet; let the spectators become an entertainment to themselves; make them actors themselves. . . .
>
> —Jean-Jacques Rousseau

---

scapes, radar-directed bombings, polar expeditions, or lunar flagraisings. Deserters and impostors, drop-outs and schizophrenics have become recog-nizable models of heroic innocence, violating the law but not everyone's cannons of justice. We can stay close to home to see well-plotted lives that have become unreal, not to be mourned when finished, not suitable for conventional movies or novels. "Straight lines are monsters," we might all chant with Delacroix if we still cared to remember him saying it. Plots, sequences, endings, frames, and instruments have been broken and scattered to make room for individuals as unmoved movers, protean in their encounter with an ever-yielding reality, able to escape the confinements the past imposes on the future. No end is fated. We deliver ourselves to chance and become willing victims with nothing to lose but our guilt. We cheerfully obliterate monuments and records, birth certificates and academic grades. Wanting no past to serve as index to our future, we are determined to make it easy to get into and out of schools, careers, neighborhoods, and—who knows?—cemeteries. The frontier has beckoned and we have crossed over.

On the other side—or on *this* side but underground—we live as mere actors. Accepting the world as stage, we appreciate nothing but one another's performances. We treat nothing as fixed or resolved, as truly original or primal, as rooted or grounded, as basic or essential, as definitively real. No home—and no longing for it. Viewing all distinctions and structures as transitional, we remain in transit—but seek no destination. We act in a demythified world whose structures exist only to allow us to experience everything in terms of its opposite. We treat whatever has the misfortune to *be*—every Certified Work of Man—as if it implied more than it affirms. We work seriously at making light of all things, at making all structures of power transparent, at compelling them to yield dimensions which, the moment they become visible, lose their claim to being. We experience no endings or punch lines—only expanding and contracting contexts, fields, grounds. And *on* the ground we see but an infinity of resplendent, luminous, reverberating effects, a permanent agitation, a vibrant expanse, an endlessly fertile continuum, a profusion of appearances, a potent void.

Clearly it is hard to sustain such a world of inconsequence—and impossible to convince outsiders that there is an unacknowledged logic justifying our embracing it. If utopian speculation is based on the conviction that something substantial will be experienced in the reborn world, these reflections of mine can have no weight. After all, I am assuming that utopia can be built only on hopelessness, that the only monument we can ever claim is an effervescent present. Only by assuming we have no basis whatever for being hopeful, no ground whatever for anticipating some great society, does it at last become possible to welcome forms of action that acquire meaning in the realization of the present, in *making* the present real. Affirming the present as open, we can finally turn away from designing utopias and recognize those ways of life as best which—while they deny that anything of consequence is ahead—offer their denials so dramatically that they reveal our capacity to act and establish an inclusive community of actors.

If the members of this community should still wonder about its origins and require some sort of creation myth, if they still must appeal to a verifiable past to give credence to their present, they might use prose less measured and more dubious than mine and tell one another about one of their ancestors—an orphan at eight, an impostor, an *actor*. He had declined to be blindfolded and, what is more, he had appealed to all of the condemned to decline likewise. They had lined up (or were being lined up) and he kept talking, describing what they all saw. He spoke rather vaguely at first, then became increasingly careful and precise. Having time, he playfully tested his words to find the most telling. As he kept turning their common experience into words, the others began to assent, correct, and elaborate, establishing connections and relating feelings they hardly knew they had. Astonished and pleased, those assembled recalled their past and found ways of leaving their mark for those who would follow. Thus they diverted themselves and lived out what lives they had—minutes, days, years. While they had no choice but to let death come however it might, when they died they were worn out, for they had added to their burden by making more of their world, their time, and themselves than they had to, as much as their talents allowed.

No one knows what any of them had actually said, but because they had somehow kept talking, they resembled the judges, wardens, guards, priests,

---

The story of this book comes to this: the story it presumes to relate will not be related.

—Robert Musil

---

and executioners who were entrenched on the other side, and who, too, did not wish to have anything come to conclusions. In fact, few in authority ever had the stomach to do their job without fuss. Forever stalling, they addressed themselves elaborately to the cases at hand, and made records of their trials. They provided for appeals, paroles, postponements, complications, and distractions—all ceremonial stays of execution. Thus they, too, used up what talents they had by diverting themselves, realizing that in the end they would also be judged, enclosed, and absolved. Like their victims, they said and recorded more than they had to, though no one knows the actual words they exchanged to give meaning to the time they served.

On occasions which later became holidays, some of the guardians of authority disguised themselves, glanced across the courtyard, and risked waving in a sign of recognition.

Notes and Sources

Prefatory Note

■ Horst Bienek. *Bakunin, eine Invention*. Munich: Deutscher Taschenbuch Verlag, 1974; p. 104.

1. Richard N. Goodwin. "Reflections." *The New Yorker*, February 4, 1974; p. 86.

■ *The New Yorker*, April 26, 1976; p. 30.

Chapter 1.   The Dominant Myth (pages 3-17)

1. Norman Mailer. *Advertisements for Myself*. New York: New American Library, 1960; p. 21.

2. Irving Howe. *Literary Modernism*. New York: Fawcett, 1970; p. 40.

■ J. H. Plumb. *The Death of the Past*. New York: Macmillan, 1969; p. 40.

■ Thomas Jefferson. "Resolutions Relative to the Alien and Sedition Laws." In Paul L. Ford, ed., *The Works of Thomas Jefferson*. New York: Putnam, 1904-1905; VIII, pp. 474-475.

■ James Madison. *The Federalist*, No. 49. 1788.

3. Sheldon S. Wolin and John H. Schaar. "Is a New Politics Possible?" *New York Review of Books*, September 3, 1970; p. 3.

■ American proverb.

4. Richard Sennett and Jonathan Cobb. *The Hidden Injuries of Class*. New York: Knopf, 1972; pp. 59-62.

■ Kansas City Resident, Mrs. Gleed Gaylord. Quoted by Harper Barnes, "Kansas City Modern." *The Atlantic*, February, 1974; p. 62.

5. Stephen Toulmin. *Human Understanding*. Princeton University Press, 1972; I, pp. 13-14.

■ American expression.

Chapter 2.   The Institutional Frame (pages 18-33)

■ *The New York Times*, November 18, 1971.

■ Advertising executive. Quoted in Jerry Della Femina, *From Those Wonderful Folks Who Gave You Pearl Harbor*. New York: Pocket Books, 1971; pp. 37-38.

1. Thus Oliver Garceau has written on the American Medical Association, Philip Selznick on the Tennessee Valley Authority, Grant McConnell on the Farm Bureau, Robert Engler on the oil industry, Samuel Huntington on the Interstate Commerce Commission, Norman Kaiser and Philip Foss on governmental advisory groups, Michael Reagan on "the managed economy," Hans Morgenthau on "the new feudalism," Arthur Selwyn Miller on "the techno-corporate state," Charles Reich on "the new property," C. Wright Mills on "the theory of balance," Ralph Miliband on "the state in capitalistic society," William Domhoff on the ruling class, John Kenneth Galbraith on "the new industrial state," Seymour Melman on "Pentagon capitalism," Theodore Lowi on "interest-group liberalism," Barbara and John Ehrenreich on "the American health empire."

2. Ira Katznelson. "Antagonistic Ambiguity." *Politics and Society*, 2 (Spring, 1972); p. 331.

■ Gore Vidal. "West Point and the Third Loyalty." *New York Review of Books*, October 18, 1973; p. 24.

3. Virginia Held. *Philosophy and Political Action*. New York: Oxford University Press, 1972; pp. 118-120.

■ Andrew Hacker. *The End of the American Era*. New York: Atheneum, 1970; p. 141.

4. Alexis de Tocqueville. *Democracy in America*. New York: Harper, 1966; pp. 666-667.

■ Henry Adams. *The Education of Henry Adams*. Boston: Little, Brown, 1918; p. 494.

■ Francine du Plessix Gray. "Old Times." *New York Review of Books*, February 22, 1973; p. 21.

5. Charles Newman. *A Child's History of America*. Chicago: Swallow Press, 1973; p. 28.

■ Wilson Carey McWilliams. *The Idea of Fraternity in America*. Berkeley: University of California Press, 1973; p. 68.

■ Richard Sennett and Jonathan Cobb. *The Hidden Injuries of Class*. New York: Knopf, 1972; pp. 138-139.

■ Peter Marin. "Tripping the Heavy Fantastic." *New York Times Book Review*, February 21, 1971; p. 7.

Chapter 3.   The Search for a Workable Myth (pages 34-47)

■ Barrington Moore, Jr. *Reflections on the Causes of Human Misery*. Boston: Beacon Press, 1972; p. 131.

■ Alexis de Tocqueville. *Democracy in America*. New York: Vintage, 1945; I, p. 5.

1. Philip Rieff. "The Impossible Culture." *Encounter*, 35 (September 1970); p. 44.

■ Roger W. Smith. "Redemption and Politics." *Political Science Quarterly*, 86 (June 1971); p. 206.

■ Ernst Cassirer. *The Myth of the State*. New Haven: Yale University Press, 1946; p. 282.

■ Albert Camus. *The Plague*. New York: Knopf, 1952; p. 150.

■ *Esquire*, September 1974; p. 85.

■ John Berger. *G*. London: Weidenfeld & Nicolson, 1972; p. 104.

■ James MacGregor Burns. *Uncommon Sense*. New York: Harper, 1972; p. 181.

2. Charles Newman. *A Child's History of America*. Chicago: Swallow Press, 1973; p. 101.

■ A twenty-four-year-old female college graduate. Quoted in Clifford Adelman, *Generations: A Collage of Youthcult*. New York: Praeger, 1972; p. 91.

3. Peter Marin. "Tripping the Heavy Fantastic." *The New York Times Book Review*, February 21, 1971; p. 7.

■ Albert Goldman. *Freakshow*. New York: Atheneum, 1971; pp. 152-153.

Chapter 4. Redeeming the Reaction to Liberalism (pages 51-55)

■ Lionel Trilling. *The Liberal Imagination*. New York: Viking, 1951; p. xiii.

■ Friedrich Nietzsche. *Ecce Homo* (1908), in *Basic Writings*. New York: Modern Library, 1966; p. 728.

1. Robert E. Ornstein. *The Psychology of Consciousness*. San Francisco: W. H. Freeman, 1972; pp. 139-140.

Chapter 5. The Model of Romanticism (pages 56-73)

■ Robert Claridge. *Living With Paradoxes*. Boston: Trowbridge Press, 1919; p. 69.

1. Robert Altman. Quoted in *Newsweek*, March 11, 1974; p. 88.

■ Paul Newman. Quoted in Leonard Probst, "Talking with Paul Newman." *The Atlantic*, November 1975; p. 72.

■ Les Levine. "For Immediate Release." *Arts and the Artist*, May 1969; p. 46.

2. Pauline Kael. "Coming: 'Nashville.'" *The New Yorker*, March 3, 1975; pp. 79-84.

3. Walter Kerr. *The Silent Clowns*. New York: Knopf, 1975.

■ Harold Rosenberg. "Thoughts in Off-Season." *The New Yorker*, July 24, 1971; p. 62.

4. Hayden White. "The Culture of Criticism." In Ihab Hassan, ed., *Liberations*. Middletown, Conn.: Wesleyan University Press, 1971; p. 68.

5. Alfred Willener. *The Action-Image of Society*, tr. Alan Sheridan Smith. New York: Pantheon, 1970; pp. 264-266.

6. Erich Heller. *The Ironic German*. Boston: Little, Brown, 1958; p. 134.

■ Richard Poirier. "Norman Mailer: A Self-Creation." *The Atlantic*, October 1972; pp. 82-83.

7. Harold Rosenberg. *The De-definition of Art: Action Art to Pop to Earthwork*. New York: Horizon Press, 1972; pp. 12-13.

8. See Alfred Willener, *The Action-Image of Society*; pp. 239, 258-259.

■ Harold Rosenberg. "Set Out for Clayton!" *The New Yorker*, January 2, 1971; p. 44.

■ Robert Morris. Statement notarized November 15, 1963.

■ Michel Foucault. *The Order of Things*. New York: Pantheon, 1970; pp. 303-304, 306.

■ *The Appeal from the Sorbonne*. Thesis 29, June 13-14, 1968.

9. Morse Peckham. *The Triumph of Romanticism*. Columbia: University of South Carolina Press, 1970; pp. 279-280.

Chapter 6.   Art as Political Action (pages 74-87)

■ Author's notebook.

1. Clifford Geertz. *The Interpretation of Cultures*. New York: Basic Books, 1973; pp. 403-404.

■ Alfred Willener. *The Action-Image of Society*. New York: Pantheon, 1970; p. 277.

■ Henry David Thoreau. *Journal* (1852), vol. 3, p. 143, in *The Writings of Henry David Thoreau*. Boston: Houghton Mifflin, 1906.

■ Author's notebook.

2. Georg W. F. Hegel. *Phenomenology of Mind*. London: Allen & Unwin, 1949; pp. 249-250.

3. Henry James. "The Private Life." In *Works*. New York: Scribner, 1909; XVII, p. 227.

4. Robert Jay Lifton. *Boundaries*. New York: Random House, 1970; p. 44.

5. Friedrich Nietzsche. "Decline of Cosmological Values." In *The Will to Power*. New York: Vintage, 1968; p. 13.

6. Morse Peckham. *The Triumph of Romanticism*. Columbia: University of South Carolina Press, 1970; pp. 55-57.

■ Author's notebook.

7. Stanley Kauffmann. "Theater." *The New Republic*, December 18, 1971; p. 20.

8. Harold Rosenberg. *Art on the Edge*. New York: Macmillan, 1975.

■ Les Levine. "For Immediate Release." *Arts and the Artist*, May 1969; p. 46.

■ Karl Marx. "The Critique of Hegel's Philosophy of Right." In *Early Writings*. London: C. A. Watts, 1963; p. 47.

Chapter 7.   Directives for Action (pages 91-99)

1. Robert Jay Lifton. "Home from the War." *The Atlantic*, November 1972; p. 69.

2. Lifton; p. 58.

3. Lifton; p. 58.

4. A friend of mine, Ian Lind, would go further:

"I have a comment on the short section you have on Vietnam (Chapter 7). I don't think that you should back down and accept that under some circumstances that sense of 'reality' is necessary. I don't think that Lifton's book makes an effective counterargument—in fact, his analysis of My Lai supports your position. In terms of the atrocity of Vietnam, your point is right on—it was the 'inability to sustain the absurdity' that led to massacre. The whole situation was experienced as absurd, yet those involved knew that it *couldn't* remain that way. Impelled to create some sense of progress, of accomplishment, some concrete and accessible standards of public achievement, some sense of going somewhere, the body-count came to have great meaning. Lifton makes the mistake of calling this particular goal an 'illusion' assuming that it can somehow be differentiated from those other goals we set for ourselves (or more usually have set for us). The drive to grant some sort of meaning led to the general phenomena of body-count and the specifics of My Lai.

"One comment Lifton makes clarifies the point: 'The people didn't know what they were dying for and the guys didn't know why they were shooting them. Yet that very emptiness and absurdity served as a further impetus toward killing—toward pressing the logic of slaughter to the very end, until some kind of meaning could be squeezed from it. The illusion—the as-if situation—is pressed to the limit until one has no choice but to see it as real.' (Lifton, *Home from the War*, p. 52)

"Lifton describes the experiences of the troops prior to My Lai. They had no real combat, just meaningless deaths in ambush, from mines (possibly planted by their Korean allies), from accidents. A lot of good people died without even the consolation of heroic combat. My Lai, then, came as an opportunity to regain control, to turn someone, anyone, into that sought-after body-count. The massacre gave the whole scene, their past and present, some reality and 'sanity': it broke the tension and was a turning point for the company. 'Until now,' one veteran said, 'we were dying uselessly.' Now they had something to talk about, a recorded appearance. 'It was really something terrific. . . . How many I got . . . the record and all this other stuff. One guy was very proud of the record. It was over one hundred.' After the killing was over, they felt better—relaxed, relieved—it was so 'good' to get back to the sort of 'reality' we all have learned to handle."

■ Stephen Toulmin. *Human Understanding*. Princeton University Press, 1972; pp. 85, 133.

5. Orion White, Jr. *Psychic Energy and Organizational Change*. Beverly Hills, Calif.: Sage Publications, 1973; pp. 30-34. Quoted from a lecture at Syracuse University, 1971.

■ Friedrich Nietzsche. "Discipline and Breeding" (1887). In Walter Kaufmann, ed. *The Will to Power*. New York: Vintage, 1968; p. 513.

■ Manfred Henningsen. *Der Fall Amerika*. Munich: List Verlag, 1974; p. 254.

Chapter 8. Theaters of Operation (pages 100-124)

■ Author's notebook.

■ Friedrich Nietzsche. *The Will to Power* (1888), ed. by Walter Kaufmann. New York: Vintage Books, 1968; p. 29.

1. Martin Duberman. *Black Mountain: An Exploration in Community*. New York: Dutton, 1972; p. 41.

2. Dubermann; p. 352.

■ "Schonbeck Initiates Music Workshop." Bennington College *Quadrille*, Spring 1976; p. 3.

3. Joshua S. Horn. *Away with All Pests*. New York: Monthly Review Press, 1969; p. 62.

4. James S. Gordon. "Service before Profit." *The New Republic*, May 6, 1972; p. 25.

■ Oliver Lee. "The People of China." *Another Voice*, March 1973; p. 3.

■ Friedrich Nietzsche. *The Will to Power*, ed. Walter Kaufmann; p. 29.

5. Talcott Parsons *et al*. "The 'Gift of Life' and Its Reciprocation." *Social Research* 39 (Autumn 1972); pp. 403, 410, 413-414.

6. Richard Sennett and Jonathan Cobb. *The Hidden Injuries of Class*. New York: Knopf, 1972; p. 261.

■ American expression.

7. Franz Kafka. *The Penal Colony*. New York: Schocken, 1968; p. 29.

■ Author's notebook.

■ John Berger. *G*. London: Weidenfeld & Nicolson, 1972; p. 77.

Chapter 9.   Revolution (pages 124-128)

■ Aristide R. Zolberg. "Moments of Madness." *Politics and Society*, 2 (Winter 1972); pp. 196-197.

■ Jean-Jacques Rousseau. *Letter to d'Alembert* (1758). In *Politics and the Arts*, tr. Allan Bloom. New York: Free Press, 1960; pp. 125-126.

■ Robert Musil. *The Man without Qualities*. London: Secker & Warburg, 1953.

Index